Webs of innovation

CREATIVE STUDIES

books for the future minded

Welcome to the next generation of business

There is a new world which we can look at but we cannot see. Yet within it, the forces of technology and imagination are overturning the way we work and the way we do business.

ft.com books are both gateway and guide to this world. We understand it because we are part of it. But we also understand the needs of businesses which are taking their first steps into it, and those still standing hesitantly on the threshold. Above all, we understand that, as with all business challenges, the key to success lies not with the technology itself, but with the people who must use it and manage it.

People like you – the future minded.

See a world of business

Visit **www.ft.com** today.

Webs of innovation

the networked economy
demands new ways
to innovate

alexander loudon

PEARSON EDUCATION LIMITED

Head Office:
Edinburgh Gate
Harlow CM20 2JE
Tel: +44 (0)1279 623623
Fax: +44 (0)1279 431059

London Office:
128 Long Acre
London WC2E 9AN
Tel: +44 (0)20 7447 2000
Fax: +44 (0)20 7240 5771
Website: www.business-minds.com

First published in Great Britain in 2001

© Pearson Education Limited 2001

The right of Alexander Loudon to be identified as Author of this
Work has been asserted by him in accordance
with the Copyright, Designs and Patents Act 1988.

ISBN 0 273 65646 5

British Library Cataloguing in Publication Data
A CIP catalogue record for this book can be obtained from the British Library.

10 9 8 7 6 5 4 3 2 1

Designed by Claire Brodmann Book Designs, Lichfield, Staffs.
Typeset by Northern Phototypesetting Co. Ltd, Bolton
Printed and bound in Great Britain by Biddles Ltd, Guildford & King's Lynn

The Publishers' policy is to use paper manufactured from sustainable forests.

about the author

Alexander Loudon was one of the early employees at the London based headquarters of First Tuesday, the global entrepreneurial network, during the time that it grew to 250,000 members in over 120 cities.

Alexander also worked in Silicon Valley for Ericsson and as an independent consultant in Amsterdam and London for customers such as Twinning and iGabriel. At present, Alexander lives in London and combines consulting work with writing about the internet evolution. His writings have been published in the Netherlands, Israel and Romania. He has been quoted over the years in well-known magazines such as *The Red Herring* and *Management Team.*

Alexander studied business at the University of Groningen, UCLA and Stanford. He is a guest lecturer at the European School of Management in Oxford and a member of the Knowledge Land Foundation Think Tank.

contents

acknowledgements

Not only does this book tell about webs of innovation, it is itself the result of a web of innovation. From a few sketches on a napkin during a breakfast with an entrepreneur in Silicon Valley towards the book you're reading right now, would not have been possible without the whole web of innovation that created itself around the concept of webs of innovation.

Over 150 individuals and companies were willing to openly share their knowledge and many of them giving insights "behind the screens." My discover tour took me through several parts of the world where I was impressed by how many nice people there are. Often without even having met me before but also proving the value of true friendship, always being there for each other. A special thank you to all the persons that offered me a place to stay (in random order): Anthony Yannatta, Nicolaas Maathuis, Cody Shearer, Dirk Rabelink, Caspar Berendsen, Thomas Loudon, Marc Wesseling, Roger Sorkin, Eva Camacho, and Krishnan Sankaranarayanan.

There were many people who read parts of my manuscript or gave me input in any other way in several stages. Too many to mention all of them but also thanks to them. A special thanks to the people who thoroughly read the whole manuscript and supplied me with feedback. Thanks for that to (in random order) Sven Atterhed, Barend Sneller, Max Loudon, Peter Olsthoorn, John Browning, Guy Kawasaki, and Michiel Westermann.

But what is a book without a publisher? Nothing. Thanks to David Hart and Steward Dodd I met with Richard Stagg of Pearson. I was and am impressed by the visionary thinking of Richard Stagg that also helped me to "fine tune" my book.

Thanks to Linda Dhondy this book has made it through the numerous phases from manuscript to book and has been hugely improved thanks to the great editing of Andrew Manning.

Throughout the whole process from a rough idea in 1998 to this book in 2001 there has been one stable factor: Hans Broekhuis. His input has been invaluable giving me directions when I needed them and motivating me to keep on going. Many thanks to this special person.

Last but not least a word to my mentors: Although you don't want me to mention names you know that I mean you, when I thank you for believing in me and stimulating me to be highly unreasonable. To quote George Bernard Shaw: "The reasonable man adapts himself to the world: the unreasonable man persists in trying to adapt the world to himself. Therefore all progress depends on the unreasonable man." It's my ambition to remain highly unreasonable.

My ambition to be highly unreasonable wasn't always shared with my parents. They however have always supported me and were always available in the background wondering what my next unreasonable adventure would be. Thanks to them for being very reasonable about my unreasonable ambitions.

Enough nice words from my side. We've got to keep on building on the web of innovation of which this book is only the start. I hope you will join me in expanding this web of innovation.

foreword

Big business has always been home to a great deal of talent and the capital to back new ideas, and yet established companies have never had a good track record in dealing with immature markets. It's time for this to change.

Today, many leading companies are increasingly looking to plug themselves into innovative opportunities through internal venturing, corporate venture capital, and acquisitions.

With the arrival of the internet, with its potential to disrupt established markets with new competitors and new business models, many businesses found themselves confronted by the critical impact of successful innovation. This was not a fatal confrontation, as many in the dot com world had predicted, but market turbulence in the last few years has left few established companies without a clearer sense of the challenge to be met in getting better at radical innovation.

Radical innovation has some interesting characteristics. Industries are frequently disrupted by outsiders – outsiders from another industry or entrepreneurs that are starting a new venture. As a new player starts from scratch, often going about things in a new or different way, they are all too often underestimated. By the time the new player, the outsider, has become a serious threat to the existing players it's usually too late.

Like many such innovators Alexander Loudon is no seasoned, gray-haired executive, but I would encourage you to pay attention to his message of innovation. For me this book captures some of the major changes and challenges established companies are going through in their search for new ways to innovate with speed and experimentation.

Professor Ir. Roel Pieper,
Managing Partner, Insight Ventures

introduction

"Large companies will become dinosaurs in the new economy" was the mantra of the nineties. With the arrival of the internet, established companies were supposed to be doomed. Small and flexible companies would make established companies become obsolete – the Davids beating the Goliaths. But as e-business is becoming business as usual, this belief is being questioned by many of these small companies as they are struggling to survive. Meanwhile, there is increasing conviction that the internet has only just begun.

We've only had the first act of the internet – the internet revolution. In the second act, the internet *evolution* it is no longer a question of start-ups versus established companies as in David versus Goliath but about start-ups and established companies both doing what they are best at in *webs of innovation*, the networks around new concepts. Start-ups are helping established companies to become dot corps – David and Goliath entering the internet evolution by joining forces.

Established companies are entering these webs of innovation via internal venturing, corporate venture capital, or acquisitions. David and Goliath working together on the "new new thing."

Why this book?

Corporations think of the internet as the next new new thing. Small companies that no one had ever heard of a few years ago seemed on course to take over from established large companies, shocking them out of their comparative advantage. The common feeling was that in the "new" economy, virtual networks of small companies would hail the end of the "old" economy domination by mature companies. However, after the short-lived success of once-lauded internet companies such as Boo.com, the focus is shifting back to the question of how established, old economy companies are leveraging their assets in the online world.

Spurred by a desire to participate in the stock market flotation boom and keep smart employees from running into the arms of venture capitalists, large corporations are devising ways to incubate potentially lucrative products and prevent them from becoming competitors.

Though in the past large companies facilitated research and development by financing and doing it themselves, they are now beginning to realize the potential of webs of innovation as gateways to new new things. An increasing number of corporations proactively enter these webs of innovation themselves.

There seem to be three strategies currently pursued by large companies. First, some are trying to enter webs of innovation by starting a separate – often competitive – division. Procter and Gamble, for instance, started Reflect.com, Wal-Mart formed Wal-Mart.com, and there are many more examples of young, high-tech spin-offs from old, more traditional companies.

The second strategy is mergers and acquisitions. Ahold, for example, acquired Peapod. Healtheon merged with WebMD.

The third way is venture capital, of which Intel is a well-known example. In 1991, the company started its venture capital activities. In March 2001, its portfolio was worth $3.3 billion.[1]

On balance, though, there is no best way yet for mature old economy companies to enter webs of innovation. However, as these established companies do not want to miss out on the internet evolution, they are increasingly trying to do so; and how they do it will undoubtedly influence the way companies will look in the information age.

Each of the three approaches can work but it is crucial to know which suits your company. This book will tell you.

The research

This book is based on three years of research. It involved reading over 250 relevant publications and interviewing 150 thought leaders in Europe and the US such as Harvard Business School Professor Clayton Christensen, former ICANN Chairman Esther Dyson, former Apple evangelist and Garage.com founder Guy Kawasaki, Nokia Venture Partners Partner John Malloy, and many others.

Over time I met with (or exchanged e-mails with) executives at Cisco, Ericsson, Philips, Panasonic, Hewlett Packard, Siemens, academics at Babson College, Stanford, Sloan School of Management, Harvard Business School, Cambridge University, Stockholm School of Economics, Rotterdam School of Management, UC Berkeley, partners at venture capital companies like Atlas Ventures and Advanced Technology Partners, consultants from the Boston Consulting Group, Arthur D Little and Strategos, lawyers from Gray Cary Ware Friedenrich, start-ups working with established companies that want to remain anonymous, influential informal investors, journalists of the Red Herring and Tornado-Insider, independent research institutes such as the Institute of the Future, financial analysts such as BT Alex Brown, independent consultants and probably many others that I have forgotten. The above list is far from complete but gives you an indication of the breadth of the research.

I combine the insights obtained from working since 1995 in the TMT (Technology Media Telecommunications) industry in the Netherlands, Silicon Valley and the UK with the theoretical research I carried out for my thesis.

To test my ideas, I used my findings at lectures I gave at universities in the Netherlands and the UK. I also organized and attended workshops relating to the subject in Europe and the US. Exclusive high profile conferences in the industry such as ETRE and the Global Internet Summit allowed me to test drive my ideas by pitching them to attending thought leaders. My monthly column on the internet evolution that is published in several countries provided me with another platform through which to verify my ideas.

The final product – this book – is the result of a thorough research and input of leading thought leaders. It is actually the result of a web of innovation that I created around a concept. By making sure that top-notch players participated in it, I hope that I have succeeded in creating some interesting reading for you.

The structure of the book

I have tried to have the structure reflect the order of my findings. Chapter 1 discusses the threat of becoming a dinosaur that established companies face. These companies could be made obsolete by missing the next wave in their industry. The inability of established companies to deal with immature markets seems to be the problem. Chapter 1 then elaborates on how immature markets differ from mature markets in the sense that innovation in immature markets is a networked process.

Chapter 2 looks at the internet revolution and how we are now getting into the internet evolution, in which the established companies, once predicted to become obsolete, are striking back. Instead of reversing the power from the start-ups to the established companies these two join forces in helping established companies to become dot corps via networked innovation.

Chapters 3, 4, and 5 elaborate on how the established companies are striking back in the internet evolution as they try to become dot corps. In chapter 3, I discuss the internal venturing programs established companies are increasingly setting up with Lucent as a case study example. As the chapter explains, this is difficult and therefore some established companies are using the services of external companies to set up their internal ventures.

Chapter 4 looks at how established companies use corporate venture capital to make sure they do not miss out on next waves and to ensure future growth by investing in start-ups with Nokia as a case study example. The chapter also explores the challenges of corporate venture capital and how to structure it.

Chapter 5 discusses how companies are increasingly acquiring soft assets such as talented employees, technical innovation, and next generation products, with Cisco as a case study example.

Chapter 6 examines how established companies, such as Volvo and Nokia, are structuring the networked innovation activities that are discussed in Chapters 3–5 and I will argue that an increasing number of them are putting their networked innovation activities in one organizational unit called a *networked innovation node*.

In Chapter 7, I take a step back and look at the wider perspective. It might be that networked innovation nodes are just the first step of a new organizational structure – established companies as webs.

At the end of each chapter are *Key points*, a number of questions which aim to help you to reflect on things learned and to apply this to your company.

The website

Just as we are at the "end of the beginning" of the internet, reading this book should be the end of the beginning of your learning experience on webs of innovation. At **www.websofinnovation.com** you can find links to relevant articles and books. There is also a mailing list, relating to each chapter, allowing you to discuss the subject with other interested readers. Over time I plan to publish presentations and other resources on this site. It's still a concept, however – it's up to you to join me and make this a successful web of innovation. You can send ideas and suggestions for the website to **alexander@websofinnovation.com**.

Notes

1. Williams, Molly. "Corporate Venture Capital Cools Off," *Wall Street Journal Europe*, July 5, 2001.

one

[the struggle of established
companies and immature markets]

IMAGINE THAT IT IS 1975 AND THREE PEOPLE WALK INTO YOUR office to propose a deal. "We've come up with a new idea of idea management that's going to change the world," says one of them, a 21-year-old guy. "Yeah sure thing," you think. Three hippie-types – long haired and unshaven. They are obviously inexperienced, and quite frankly you consider them to be a bunch of weirdos. They don't even have a business plan. The only thing they do have is a prototype, but they have no idea how to build or sell it.

You also know that so far, of all the people they have met with nobody has bought into their ideas. Take for instance Joe Keenan, President of Atari. When they offered his company the rights to their product he replied "Get your feet off my desk, get out of here, you stink, and we're not going to buy your product."

How would you have responded? Consider the factors – an inexperienced management team, no business plan, no partnerships, no other investors yet, and so on. They meet almost none of the standard requirements for a successful company. So, how did these guys end up? They did pretty well. The company was named Apple and developed the world's first personal computer. In July 2001 the company had a market cap of $7.8 billion.

Was this unique? Not at all. There are numerous similar examples. The key thing is that something new tends to be beyond the paradigm that people use in a mature market for their analysis and, therefore, this new thing is often rejected. The problem though is that this innocent looking new thing one day might become the way things are and make established players or complete industries obsolete.

Do radical new ideas get a chance in your organization? How can you organize your organization to allow for innovation without losing sight of today's performance?

Most of the companies were built with the assumption that their business models were immortal but with the arrival of the internet, things are changing. Supply chains are restructured, new large players have arrived, for some transactions the costs have dropped significantly because of more efficient processes – and this is just the beginning. We've had the internet revolution and now it's time for the internet *evolution*. Not that much has changed yet but – as with other disruptive technologies – over time we will be starting to find out the great things the internet brings as the "information age" progresses.

How can your company innovate its way into this information age? This book aims to show you how – via starting and structuring internal venturing, corporate venture capital, or acquisitions – established

companies are entering webs of innovation, the networks around new concepts, to become dot corps.

Established companies used to struggle with innovation in immature markets but it now seems that established companies are increasingly discovering how to ensure that they do not miss out on next waves by entering webs of innovation. It seems as though now we've managed to master quality, mastering innovation is the next challenge. In this chapter I discuss why established companies have a hard time dealing with immature markets and how these immature markets work, moving on to how the internet revolution is transitioning into an internet evolution and how established companies are working on becoming dot corps by entering webs of innovation.

The threat of becoming a dinosaur

The PC example

Do you remember Commodore, VisiCalc, MicroPro, and Tandy? They were *the* players in the personal computer (PC) industry 20–25 years ago. PCs were perceived as expensive toys and large companies stuck to mainframes and minicomputers. These days not too much is left from the companies that ruled 20–25 years ago. However, the PC industry did not come to an end. On the contrary, these days it is hard to imagine life without PCs. New players such as IBM, Microsoft, Ashton-Tate, and Lotus changed the PC from an expensive tool to an affordable tool for the masses with the operating system MS Windows, database program dBase II and spreadsheet program Lotus 1-2-3. Via small and mid-sized companies, which could not afford mainframes and minicomputers, the PC made it into the mainstream market thanks to this useful software.

Think about which of players in the will still be

it for a second: the **current** internet industry around in

20–25 years' time?

Some say the same is about to happen in the internet industry. We're still in a very early stage finding out about applications besides e-mail and the browser that are going to make our lives faster, better, and cheaper. (This is explored further in Chapter 2.) Think about it for a second; which of the current players in the internet industry will still be around in 20–25 years' time?

More about the internet later. For now, it is interesting to observe that the pattern always seems to be the same. A mature market with a clear leader in which a new player, or an existing one from a different market, introduces a radical innovation. As this innovation is not perfect (yet), it is not taken seriously. The participants in the web of innovation, the network that is on the basis of the new idea, develops an advantage by being ahead because of the learning process it has been through and the former market leader misses out. Professor Clayton Christensen of Harvard wrote a bestseller about this: *The Innovators Dilemma*. He calls this type of radical innovations "disruptive technologies."

Enough examples. Digital had a hard time in the eighties when it did not take the rise of the PC seriously and IBM did. IBM, however, had the same experience when Compaq could offer computers at very competitive prices because of its efficient business model. Dell surprised Compaq itself with its internet-based business model.

Once again, change is looming in the PC market. It is no longer the case that personal computers are mostly manufactured by Compaq and Dell, running Microsoft applications powered by Intel chips and connected by Cisco networks to Oracle and Sun databases.[1]

Changing strategies

As the emphasis moves from the desktop to the network these companies are all adjusting their strategy. Microsoft for instance is introducing .Net, allowing interoperability between different hardware and software applications across multiple platforms. Some say Microsoft is too late, while others say that Microsoft caught up with the web browser as well. When Netscape introduced its web browser in 1994 Microsoft did not take it too seriously. However, in 1995 Microsoft changed its opinion and formed a team dedicated entirely to developing the web browser. This move paid off as Microsoft gradually picked up market share. These days more people use Microsoft's web browser Explorer than Netscape's Navigator. Others say that Microsoft will fail as it has not structured the .Net activities as a separate group and therefore there will be conflicts with existing business managers as they perceive the .Net activities as a threat to their business. At Microsoft, tensions are already rising between existing business managers and new business managers. For example, a group creating a new web word processing and calendaring system called Netdocs is facing resistance from the group that runs the nearly $10 billion a year Office business.[2]

New players tackle established companies

Meanwhile new players such as Juniper, Linux, and Transmeta are emerging and taking on the established companies such as Cisco, Microsoft, and Intel.

Juniper versus Cisco

Cisco sells routers (the traffic agents for the internet) and the company has been very successful at this. In its early days the company was the start-up that was taking it up against established telecom players such as Nortel and Lucent. However, as the company is maturing, that is changing. One of the biggest threats for Cisco these days is Juniper. This company started in 1996 with a management composed of former vice presidents of well known telecommunications companies such as

Bay Networks, Stratacom, Cisco, and others, backed by an impressive number of bluechip companies such as AT&T from Ericsson Inc., Lucent Technologies, Nortel (Northern Telecom), the Siemens/Newbridge alliance, 3Com Corporation, and Worldcom Inc.'s subsidiary UUNET Technologies Inc., Juniper sells fast routers and was faster to market with the super-fast 10-gigabit router than Cisco. Part of Juniper's successful recipe is that it binds together four slower processors to achieve a higher speed. As a typical market leader Cisco responded arrogantly by describing the Juniper router as "strapping together four Volkswagens and calling it a Porsche."[3]

Analysts estimate[4] however, that Juniper captured 35 percent of the $2 billion-plus core router market by the end of 2000. That would leave Cisco having 65 percent of the market. This figure might sound great but that's down from 75 percent. Sounds familiar doesn't it? A new player that outperforms the existing monopolist in a niche market and might make the existing monopolist obsolete.

Linux versus Micrsoft

Operating system (OS) Linux is taking on Microsoft. Started by a 21-year-old Finnish student in 1991 called Linus Torvalds, this OS is used by millions of people and organizations worldwide. What makes it interesting is that the software is not proprietary, which is why it is called "open source" software. Instead of the traditional intellectual property approach by software companies to write software in-house and make money by selling it under copyrights and releasing improved versions every few years (take for instance Microsoft's releases of new versions of Windows) the open source movement preaches releasing the program's "core," being the source code, to the public and that way having programmers from all over the world working on and improving the code and program. For Linux for instance, new versions are released every month. The major advantages are that new versions are released much faster and tend to be of a better quality. The program is developed continuously by a group of over 100 supportive developers. Torvalds combines his day job at a start-up with co-ordinating the development of Linux.

The reason for its popularity is that Linux is reliable and free. As the operating system is "lighter" than, for example, Windows it runs fine on older, and therefore cheaper, computers. In 1998 researchers at Los Alamos National Laboratory used Linux to run 68 PCs as a single parallel processing machine to simulate atomic shock waves. Including labor this homemade supercomputer cost only $152,000 – about one-tenth of the price of a comparable commercial machine at the time. For that money they had the 315th fastest computer in the world.[5]

Linux is mostly run on servers, the computers that form networks. It is rarely used with desktops as the development of graphical user interfaces is at an early stage. However, this is being worked on and Linus Torvalds has also announced that he is working on a version of Linux for mobile devices, a "hot" area as growth in that market is forecast. Windows proprietary OS Windows versus Linux open source OS resembles the "Apple versus IBM" situation according to some commentators. In an internal memorandum leaked to the Open Source movement in October 1998 Microsoft stated its view of the threat very clearly: "…OSS [Open Source Software] poses a direct, short-term revenue and platform threat to Microsoft, particularly in server space. Additionally, the intrinsic parallelism and free idea exchange in OSS has benefits that are not replicable with our current licensing model and therefore present a long-term developer mindshare threat."

Transmeta versus Intel

Intel is taken on by Transmeta. Transmeta has developed a microprocessor that uses less energy than the microprocessors of

Intel and Advanced Micro Devices (AMD). What makes it so interesting is that it uses less energy than is currently common. It is also cheaper and stays cooler than the processors of competitors such as Intel or Advanced Micro Devices (AMD). In addition, Transmeta's microprocessor is especially designed for use in laptops and "dedicated appliances" such as personal digital assistants (PDAs). An enormous growth market therefore. Behind the scenes Transmeta has obtained commitment from an impressive series of companies such as Sony, Casio, Fujitsu, NEC, Gateway, and America Online (AOL).

The skeptics state that Transmeta's Crusoe is slower than the best processors of Intel and AMD. Besides that Intel is expected to release a processor using less energy as well. The processor is not the only place in a laptop where energy use can be reduced. Transmeta has had to recall some products as the processors in NECs laptop had faults in them. In case these problems turn out to be "child diseases" and the skeptics are wrong, then Transmeta's technology could become a "disruptive technology" and that way the company could become the new Intel.

It will be interesting whether the established companies will be able to catch the networking wave or whether they will slowly become "dinosaurs," allowing the previously mentioned companies and other new players to take over.

TABLE 1.1 New leaders in the networking wave?

From	To
Cisco	Juniper
Microsoft	Linux
Intel	Transmeta

Responding to innovation

When looking at Transmeta and Juniper it is interesting to see that the founding management have mainly worked at established players in the respective markets, such as Sun, Intel, and Cisco, prior to starting or joining their current companies. That seems to be a pattern. People who used to work at an established company are quite often behind successful start-ups. Research by Professor Bhide of the Harvard Business School found that about 71 percent of successful start-ups he surveyed replicated or modified an idea encountered through previous employment.[6] The employer usually refused to execute the idea because of either the fear of cannibalizing existing products, or the product did not fit within the existing line of products. As a result, the budding entrepreneur left the organization to execute his or her idea. Many opportunities have been lost in this way. One of the most well-known examples is Xerox with its Palo Alto Research Center (Xerox PARC) during the seventies and eighties in Silicon Valley.

Xerox PARC is known as a research center from which many innovations originated. Take for instance Ethernet, which local area networks are based on. The idea was born at Xerox PARC. As Bob Metcalfe could not convince the management about the great business potential of the product he decided to leave in order to start his own company. In 1979 he worked from his Palo Alto apartment and incorporated from there as 3Com. Nowadays the company has a market cap of $2.2 billion (May 2001).

Xerox is not alone. An increasing number of established companies are seeing the importance of catching the next wave, and trying to find the most effective way to deal with it. In practice, this is hard and a magic formula has not yet been found. Recognizing what could be disruptive is an art that most established companies are starting to master, although many of them are finding out that the next step – growing disruptive ideas and bringing them to the market – is hard. Things that have a potential to radically change business as usual cannot be managed as business as usual. Skeptics say that it is impossible and that companies automatically fall into a defensive response of defending their company by improving existing business instead of giving the disruptive stuff a chance. But hey, that's what they also said about quality.

When the first ideas about quality management were suggested, everybody thought they were crazy but it is now part of business life. The same will happen to the management of innovation. Now we have succeeded in mastering quality management it seems that innovation is the next big challenge. Innovation has been the buzzword in annual reports of established companies as the importance of innovation within the strategic renewal of companies becomes increasingly clear. It is interesting that it is not only a buzzword. Established companies are working hard on "walking the talk." Interesting patterns of ways to master innovation are arising as an increasing number of established companies are trying to avoid missing the new new thing by starting and/or further structuring internal venturing programs, corporate venture capital funds and acquisitions, in order to ensure being part of the right webs of innovation. Some are even creating separate structures within their organization called networked innovation nodes (see Chapter 6).

Now we have succeeded in mastering quality management it seems that innovation is the next big challenge.

These activities were especially kick started with the arrival of the internet, one of the biggest disruptive technologies of the 20th century. Established companies missed out at the first wave of the internet; the internet revolution. As we will find out in Chapter 2 the internet is just starting, so offering established companies a chance to strike back in the second wave of the internet – the internet evolution. We're just at the start of experiencing the impact of the internet. What it has achieved so far is to make businesses aware of the importance of entrepreneurship and innovation as new players arose from scratch in the market such as eBay, an online auction site. Many employees left established companies to set up companies and that way created significant value in some cases of which their previous employers had no share. This woke up established companies and made them aware that they should not miss the next wave of value creation by the internet.

While everybody was focusing on continuous improvement, the internet woke us up and made established organizations aware of the importance of *strategic renewal* in order to keep a competitive advantage. "Six Sigma," Total Quality Management, Kaizen, and re-engineering helped out on continuous improvement. That's great for maintaining existing businesses, but what if a new business comes up that might turn the business around drastically or even make the existing one become obsolete? It is great to be a market leader but what is the point if that market is made obsolete? The internet makes companies consider the question: "What will help us out to manage innovation in a structured way without losing sight of today's performance?" An old corporate dilemma. How can you evoke missing out on the next wave in a structured way while continuing to be a market leader in the existing business? (See Figure 1.1.)

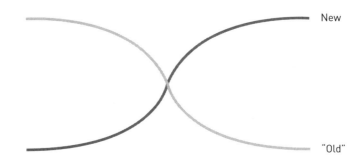

New

"Old"

FIGURE 1.1 The corporate dilemma of strategic renewal

This is complicated as old and new business require different structures. Later in this chapter, we will find out how established companies are dealing with immature markets via networked innovation. The coming chapters will elaborate on the key components of networked innovation – internal venturing, corporate venture capital and acquisitions. Chapter 6 reveals how established companies are separating networked innovation activities in so-called "networked innovation nodes." More about that later.

Back to the corporate dilemma of strategic renewal. Somehow established companies seem to be good at conducting their business in existing and mature markets but immature markets are another story. The management ideas that work fine in mature markets seem not to apply in immature markets. That is dangerous as these immature markets will one day mature and might make other markets become obsolete. Let's elaborate a bit on the differences between mature and immature markets before we get a bit more into depth on immature markets.

Mature versus immature markets

From little acorns ...

In immature market innovation tends to be learning by doing. You start from scratch with a vision and take it from there. The focus is on product innovation – creating your product or service. As the market matures, the focus moves to process innovation – improving your product or service and the processes around it.[7] By the way, the ideas presented in this book apply to both products *and* services; for ease of use I will stick to using the word "product" to mean both.

Usually the first version of a product is not perfect as you learn by doing in immature markets. As Silicon Valley guru Guy Kawasaki says: "Don't worry, be crappy." Think for instance about Windows. How good was Windows 3.0? Far from perfect but it was there and got a lot of people hooked up. Following versions provided its users with improvements. The majority of computers nowadays run on a Windows operating system.

Jeff Hawkins, the guy behind the PalmPilot, one of the first personal digital assistants, carved out the prototype from a piece of wood. Story goes that he walked around with it and used it as if it was already working to try whether it felt natural. He wanted to create a device, which one could easily carry around and which was intuitively, fast, reliable, and simple to use. The next step he took was investigating what technologies were needed. It turned out that it used a 20-year-old processor, 128kb RAM working memory and a basic operating system. Nothing radically new. The only new thing needed was an input technology. But Hawkins had already developed that at his previous employer, General Magic. The first PalmPilot was really basic but over

Neither
Palmcomputing
PalmPilot
reached their
without taking
first version of
and developing

Microsoft nor with the could have current position a very basic their product it over time.

time the company released improved versions. Right now the newest model will have a full-colour screen and will also have phone functionalities. Nowadays the PalmPilot still dominates the market. In 2000 its market share in the US was 72.1 percent.[8]

Neither Microsoft with Windows nor Palmcomputing with the PalmPilot could have reached their current position without taking a very basic first version of their product and developing it over time.

Another Silicon Valley guru, Geoff Moore, wrote a book *Crossing the chasm* about the transition from immature to mature markets in the high tech market that has led to a standard marketing vocabulary in Silicon Valley among venture capitalists and entrepreneurs. Moore's ideas are now also becoming popular among established companies outside the high tech market as established companies are trying to become dot corps. His most interesting finding is that the hardest part with growing a new product is changing the customer base from the nerds who want to have newest cool products towards the average member of the public who simply buy the product because it makes their lives easier. A lot of products fail to succeed because of missing this transition, which Moore refers to as "the chasm." After this transition the real profits start. Companies that have successfully crossed the chasm are Microsoft, Nokia, and Intel.

Innovation or efficiency?

Whereas Moore focuses on the marketing side of differences between mature and immature markets, there is also an organizational side to it. Business in mature markets is managed in a different way than business in immature markets. In mature markets companies tend to take the product or service as given and focus on improving it and the processes around it. The emphasis moves from innovation to efficiency. Assuring a dominant position by making sure you have the smartest people working for you and taking all possible measures to protect your intellectual property. Innovation becomes a linear process. In this process, innovation moves in a formal way from the left to the right beginning with basic research, progressing sequentially through fixed and sequential stages of product development, production and marketing, and terminating with the successful sale of new products and services.[9] Because the majority of the variables are known, these steps can be planned and a budget allocated. As the goal is to make existing things better, it is clear which part of the business is involved, which staff it concerns, and what the goals are. This is completely opposite to innovation in immature markets where the majority of variables are unknown and discovered "on the fly." In immature markets, innovation is not a linear process but an iterative one – learning by doing.

FIGURE 1.2 The linear process of innovation in mature markets

Example: the US ice industry

Many companies in mature markets tend to place so much emphasis on *efficiency* that they forget to keep on innovating. This is what can make major players become dinosaurs and there are many examples of how once major players were made obsolete by losing sight of the need for innovation. Although they remained market leader for their product, the product was replaced by another one making the leadership worthless. My favorite example is that of the ice industry in the Northeast of the US, described below.

In the late 1800s the Northeast of the US had a successful ice industry. Ice blocks were cut from frozen lakes and ponds and sold around the world. Ships were used to transport the ice. Although generally, half of the shipment melted during the transport the other half was enough to make a profit.

The companies that innovated mechanical icemakers put these ice harvesters out of business. Because of that innovation cutting and shipping of ice was no longer necessary since it was now possible to make ice anywhere and at any time.

While this ice-making business started to boom, another radical innovation came into place, that of the refrigerator. People now could just make ice and store it at home. Now in turn, the icemakers were put out of business.

Do not overlook the need to innovate

The above example shows how easily major players can become dinosaurs by focusing on efficiency and overlooking the need to innovate. Companies are becoming increasingly aware of this threat and are figuring out ways to enter these webs of innovation that are on the basis of immature markets while continuing their existing mature business.

Immature markets seem to be something completely different – starting from scratch and learning by doing. This is the opposite from innovation in mature markets where it is a linear process that moves from the left to the right in fixed and sequential stages with a focus on improving existing business. There are numerous examples of companies that were made obsolete by ignoring immature markets and thereby missing the next wave.

The internet is an immature market around which several webs of innovation are emerging. The challenge for the established companies will be to see these webs come up and become part of right ones. Established companies seem to have mastered quality and now the next challenge is entering webs of innovation. As you will find out in the coming chapters, established companies are increasingly structuring the way they enter webs of innovation.

To avoid becoming dinosaurs, established companies should make sure that they foresee emerging webs of innovation and participate if they want to become dot corps. To do that they should first develop an understanding of how webs of innovation develop themselves around concepts.

It's about concepts
Immature markets start around concepts around which players plug themselves into. It is not without reason that venture capitalists usually prefer it if there are three or more other companies working on the same idea. That way they get market validation for their idea as it is clear that a new web of innovation is being formed and several participants in the web are trying to create a business out of it.

Consider, for example, the rise of the commercial internet incubators in Europe. Around the end of 1999, they were suddenly the new new thing. These were companies helping dot com start-ups to start up their start-up. The incubator would offer their services to start-ups in exchange for a stake in the company. This stake varied between 10 percent and 70 percent of the company. The perception in the market was that in Europe there was a lack of people with experience and a network in the internet industry. Incubators would fill this gap by offering both of these. In January 1999 there was about a handful of them in Europe – by January 2000 there were several hundred in Europe. Everybody wanted to invest in an incubator hoping that a new Cisco or eBay would be incubated and make them very rich. Venture capitalists and investment banks were waiting in line to invest in an incubator. Several incubators, such as Brainspark, were floated even though they were less than a year old and had not proved themselves.

Once the initial internet hype was over, many incubators have either failed or became holding companies as they ran short of money. The business models were based on quick "exits" of incubees by going public. After the hype it takes a while before you can take a company public. Sometimes the (in theory, perfect) models of standardizing the path from idea to exit did not work out and the incubees became failures. In addition, the cost of keeping the operations going is high.

These incubators are little more than start-ups themselves. They are not so different from their incubees – they have just received funding and are still refining their business model and have to prove themselves. The proving will be in how many of their companies will make it to the next round of financing. In the future, an expected shake-out and consolidation will show which ones have a sustainable business model. London-based New Media Spark, for example, acquired Stockholm-based Cell Ventures in 2000. Another London-based incubator, E-Souk's lay-off of 22 of its 29 employees in 2000 was another sign of restructuring in the industry. When I asked Christopher Spray of Atlas Ventures how many incubators will be left in a few years he told me: "probably a few per country and pan-European, in any case not the number we see now."

Nevertheless it's an interesting example. A concept develops, in this case that of the incubator, and suddenly everybody wants to be involved even though the business models are not clear yet and haven't proven themselves; even now many incubators are still refining their own business models and there has been no proof of the concept in Europe. Meanwhile a shake-out and consolidation is going on.

The pattern always seems to be the same. To the outside world it seems that suddenly a whole network of customers, competitors, and partners around a certain idea, a web of innovation, comes into existence. Many players try to jump in the web and try to create a business out of the concept. As the market matures a shake-out occurs resulting in a decrease in the number of players in the web of innovation. Besides the shake-out, consolidation also occurs in the industry, reducing the number of players. At the end only a few players remain.

Do you know how many producers of white plastic disposable cups there are in the US? Five. Why? Because it is very hard to make and sell these white plastic disposable cups. Even though the idea is simple, building a good company takes time. Coming up with a good idea happens easily, building a company costs time.

To catch the next wave established companies need to predict new webs of innovation and enter the right ones to avoid becoming dinosaurs. These webs of innovation seem to evolve over a certain pattern. Immature markets start with a concept around which a network involving customers, competitors and partners evolves, many players come into existence trying to make a business out of it and after a shake-out and consolidation, only a few survive. This is the pattern in the internet industry as I will describe in Chapter 2. The challenge for established companies is to enter these webs of innovation in time if they want to become dot corps.

Innovating = networking

It is interesting to note that it is not research but the generation of a concept that is the basis of innovation in immature markets. It all seems to happen within a web of innovation. So it is not the individual organization that is at the center but the web of innovation. Therefore seeing new webs of innovation at an early stage and making sure to enter the right ones in time is essential for established companies if they want to catch the next wave – a completely different approach to that required in mature markets. Within a web of innovation several parties are involved. Your customers, partners, and even your competitors. It's a process that takes place in a network, so I would like to call the process of innovation in immature markets "networked innovation."

As CEO and President of Cisco, John Chambers said in an e-mail to me:[10] "You bring up an interesting point about mature markets versus immature markets.... [networked innovation] includes partnering, acquisitions and internal and external investments as the goal is to be best in class at various levels and to create an 'ecosystem' of partners."

Although the mantra in the nineties used to be that "Large companies will become dinosaurs in the new economy," it turns out that in practice these webs of innovation are quite often centered around an established company. It's not about networks of small companies beating the established companies – both start-ups and established companies are becoming increasingly aware of their strengths and weaknesses. Start-ups are good at *exploring* and established companies are better at *exploiting*. Smart established companies acknowledge the importance of being in the center of webs of innovation and are proactive in being in that position.

Hewlett Packard (HP) has its so-called "scanning units." These are small and flexible teams of two to four marketing and technical experts who spend their time talking with current, former, and potential customers to scan the market for new webs of innovation. They match these opportunities with the internal capabilities and create a map of

It's not about networks of small companies beating the established companies – **both** start-ups and established companies are becoming **increasingly aware of their** strengths and weaknesses. Start-ups are good at *exploring* and established companies are better at *exploiting*.

innovation targets, after which they screen these targets against ten HP critical success factors.[11]

It seems though that empowering the customer is not the only thing to do. This empowering of the customer can have its problems as well. A lot of mature market players try to listen to the customer, because very well-paid gurus and consultants tell them to – often correctly when it's about improving business in mature markets. However, it should not be the only thing companies base their offerings on. If they only focus on listening to the customer, companies miss new innovations because they're *following* the customer instead of serving the customer by being one step ahead. Given the fact that sometimes technologies progress faster than market demand as Professor Clayton Christensen describes so well in his book[12] this can lead to being left behind by missing the learning advantage that competitors or new players who moved on time have had.

New players often enter the market via niches. Think of how the PC entered the market. While minicomputer manufacturer Digital saw the

PCs emerging, it did not view them as a serious threat as its customers at that time didn't take the PC seriously. However, via useful applications for small and mid-sized companies the PC entered the mainstream market. Where would Digital be if they had entered the PC web of innovation in time?

Even the competition gets involved in webs of innovation. An interesting example is IBM. This company builds computers as well as selling components. In the latter role it sells vital parts to PC manufacturer Dell. For IBM it is essential to have access to detailed specifications and business process information of Dell. Dell has based the majority of its logistics and planning on IBM delivery capacity. It is a strong collaboration although the companies are also competitors.[13] It is not about cycles of co-operation, competition, co-operation – but about simultaneous co-operation and competition. Professors Brandenburg and Nalebuff coined the term "co-opetition" for this in their bestseller of that title.

The number of inter-firm co-operations has been growing significantly over the past 20 years as an increasing number of companies acknowledges the importance of collaboration. This is also supported by academics who found out that collaborating firms are often more innovative. Research by the STEP group for instance found that the sales of companies that collaborate on their R&D has a higher percentage of new products as part of total sales than those that do not collaborate on their R&D.[14] Established companies are increasingly acknowledging that having ideas alone is worth nothing, it really becomes something when it becomes a business. To achieve that a company has to network. Innovating is networking.

Silicon Valley is the proof of the statement that innovating is networking. Many webs of innovation started from the Valley. Stimulated by the fact that there is a lot of movement of people from firm to firm, companies have learned the importance of networking instead of isolating the company. A lot of companies in Silicon Valley simply wouldn't have been where they are now if they were not focused on being part of webs of innovation. This culture of openly sharing information relating to the business and helping each other does not exclude the competition. In webs of innovation competitors are involved as well. Whatever it takes to create a business.

Figure 1.3 shows the process of networked innovation from an established company perspective.

AnnaLee Saxenian of the University of California at Berkeley compared Route 128 (the east coast equivalent of Silicon Valley, the area nearby MIT and Harvard) with Silicon Valley in her best-selling book *Regional Advantage*. Somehow Route 128 had lost the glory it

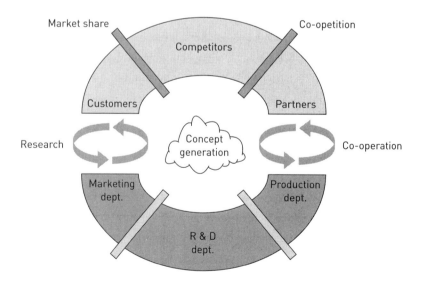

FIGURE 1.3 The process of networked innovation

had in the sixties while Silicon Valley was still an epicenter for innovation. She found that the big difference was that in Route 128 companies isolated the process of innovation to a large extent within their corporate boundaries, whereas Silicon Valley based companies worked collectively on new concepts via webs of innovation. Saxenian points at the importance of technological compatibility, shortening lead times, and strategic objectives as the key advantages. A lot of firms would have simply been unable to compete if they had not been willing to enter into a variety of forms of technological co-operation. Because of the extremely rapid pace of technical change and the broad range of specialized technological capabilities needed for system development, there was simply no time to do it alone Saxenian concludes. By entering webs of innovation these companies all created their own business within their web in which every company focuses on what it is good at.

The conventional idea of that to be successful in business you have to increase your power by weakening your competitors seems to be challenged here. In webs of innovation you share your power with your customers, your partners, and sometimes even with your competitors in case you want to succeed. By sharing your power you become part of a web of innovation that allows you to leverage and build upon the success of the other parts of the web.[15] This requires a new mindset.

Webs of innovation that form immature markets evolve via a networked process around a concept. In immature markets networking seems to be key. One could state that with networked innovation success or failure depends on the quality of the relations with other parties involved in the web of innovation. It is therefore important to align in an early stage for all participants in webs of innovation. To become dot corps established companies have to make sure that they work out the right alliances within the webs of innovation to which they belong.

Align early or get quashed PalmComputing is a good example of a company that has done well with its strategic alliances. This company is involved in a lot of alliances – Table 1.2 provides some examples.

TABLE 1.2 PalmComputing and some of its strategic alliances

Market	Partner	Alliance
Companies	IBM	IBM does OEM (original equipment manufacturing) for PalmPilot Pro and Palm III
Bar code scanning/ wireless LAN/WAN	Symbol Technologies	Industrial version with integrated bar-coding and wireless LAN (local area network/WAN (wide area network)
Time management/ personal productivity	Franklin Covey	PalmPilot bundled with Ascend

Source: PalmComputing sales presentation in Silicon Valley, 1998

The strategic alliance is increasing in popularity. This is because in the high tech market the product cycle is continuously becoming shorter and that way there's less and less time to bring a product to market.

A good example is the co-operation between Qualcomm (a cell phone manufacturer) and PalmComputing (best known for the PalmPilot), to

From a start-up

importance of

alliances is

acknowledged.

alliances with

brands is

perspective **the**

these strategic

increasingly

Having strategic

established

important **for**

start-ups.

produce the PdQ. This is an intelligent cellular phone that combines a cellular phone with a PDA.

Whether this is a PalmPilot in a Qualcomm cellular phone or a Qualcomm cellular phone in a PalmPilot is irrelevant. What matters is selling the product. You do that by getting into as many strategic alliances as needed.

From a start-up perspective the importance of these strategic alliances is increasingly acknowledged. Having strategic alliances with established brands is important for start-ups. It gives credibility that helps to get products accepted more readily.

During the internet hype a lot of dot coms announced almost every external step they took as a strategic alliance. When they bought a new server from Sun it was announced as a strategic alliance with Sun or if they bought a new license for Windows NT it was announced as strategic alliance with Microsoft. A PR professional in the Valley told me that his dot com clients send out about four times as many press releases as his other clients did. The majority of these dot com businesses had press releases almost every month to announce "strategic alliances." However, it is not all plain sailing with these strategic alliances. Many companies found out that in practice, it is not easy to make good strategic alliances. Over time it can for instance turn out that the start-up disagrees with the strategy of its alliance partner. That can lead to conflicts. That's just one example.

Good alliances take some guidelines. One fundamental guideline is that companies should take care not to have too big an overlap in products because this could slow down the process; remaining separate is key here. It seems that strategic alliances between partners with complementary skills have a greater chance of being successful.[16] Founder Jeff Hawkins of PalmPilot stated it best at a Churchill Club meeting in Silicon Valley when he stated: "Partners are great to extend out of your core technology but not within." To ensure compatibility there should also be agreement on where the industry is going and how their individual corporate strategy fits in as well as clarity on the areas in which they are going to co-operate and those where they will continue to compete is also evident.

The GSM example

Another important reason for aligning early is that as new ideas are developed in webs of innovation, standards are also set. An example is the GSM standard that was set in Europe.

In 1982 the development of a digital cellular standard began, initiated by Nordic Telecom and KPN Telecom of the Netherlands. In 1987 a group of about 13 operators and administrators formed a regulating institute called Groupe Specialisé Mobile. The group drafted a specification and in 1989 the European Telecommunications Standards Institute defined GSM (named after the group) as the internationally accepted digital telephony standard. GSM further developed via annual conferences and was later renamed to Global System for Mobile Communications. Meanwhile a lot of players entered the market both from the infrastructure builders side as well as from the infrastructure exploiters side. Nowadays about 700 GSM mobile networks have been established all over the world, the majority of them woven together by international roaming agreements.[17] The early setting of standards permitted this rapid growth. All the players that entered the GSM web of innovation in time could profit from the agreed sets of standard and that way be fast in developing their products.

Due in particular to increasingly shorter and fast product cycles, alliances are becoming popular. In an interview, Silicon Valley based venture capitalist Jos Henkens knows that: "If you don't align yourself early, you'll get quashed." The strategic alliance as a way to hook up with a web of innovation and get a product faster to market, by setting the standards, reducing uncertainty and sharing costs and knowledge.

Webs of innovation come into existence via a process of networked innovation around a certain concept. Networking is therefore key and established companies should align early in the next wave of the internet to make sure that they don't miss out this time and can become dot corps.

Conclusion

Established companies are confronted with the problem that their current success is based on their existing business. While growing their existing business they should also be aware of immature markets that are emerging. Managing an existing business in an efficient way and meanwhile innovating your way into new business is the corporate dilemma many established companies struggle with. The emphasis often tends to be on efficiency and not on innovation.

Innovation in immature markets is different from innovation in mature markets – in immature markets the focus is on product innovation, coming up with new things, and in mature markets the focus is on process innovation, making existing things better.

Immature markets seem to evolve via webs of innovation, centered around a concept. These webs of innovation are networks of companies, customers, competitors, and partners, formed around a concept. Within webs of innovation it is essential to align yourself early, otherwise you get quashed. Smart established companies try continuously to be part of webs of innovation or even smarter to create them. It seems that now we've mastered the art of managing quality the next challenge will be managing innovation by entering webs of innovation.

In immature markets the focus is on product innovation and in mature markets the focus is on process innovation.

With this knowledge in mind, Chapter 2 examines one of the most disruptive technologies of the 21st century – the internet. After the internet revolution, the internet evolution is the next step. Chapter 2 also shows how established companies are starting and/or structuring networked innovation activities so that they do not miss out on the relevant webs of innovation in the internet evolution and can become dot corps.

Key points

 Is your company staying ahead of the customer or following behind?

 In which webs of innovation is your company involved? In which webs should it be involved but isn't?

 Are customers, competitors, and partners involved in your company's innovation processes?

 What percentage of your company's annual revenues comes from new products (less than five years old)?

 With which competitors do you or could you collaborate?

Consider any recent disruptive technologies that affected your industry. What happened and how did your company respond?

Think of a successful innovation. How did it start?

 When is being an established company an advantage and when is being a start-up an advantage?

 Are there organizational structures, investments, and incentives in place in your organization for both efficiency and innovation in your organization? If this is the case what is the emphasis on? When the emphasis is on efficiency, what would it take to put a similar emphasis on innovation?

 Why do some established companies stop growing at some point?

 Is your business active in an immature or mature market? If both, is the balance right?

Further information

At the website **www.websofinnovation.com** you can find additional resources on the subject, such as links to relevant articles, books, websites and over time this will be expanded. A mailing list on the subject of this chapter allows you to discuss it with other readers.

Notes

1. Lynn, Matthew. "Wired to Wireless," *Business 2.0*, UK edition, Christmas 2000.

2. Greene, Jay. "Microsoft's big bet," *Business Week*, October 30, 2000, McGraw Hill Group.

3. Files, Jennifer. "Cisco answers Juniper's challenge," *San Jose Mercury News*, January 30, 2000.

4. Ibid.

5. McHugh, Josh. "For the love of hacking," *Forbes*, August 10, 2000.

6. Bhide, Amar. "The origin and evolution of new businesses," Oxford University Press, Oxford, UK 2000.

7. Utterback, James. *Mastering the dynamics of innovation*, Harvard Business School Press, Boston, MA 1996.

8. Tam, Pui-Wing. "Market for hand-held PCs doubled in US last year." *Wall Street Journal Europe*, January 26, 2001.

9. Organization for Economic Co-operation and Development (OECD). "Technology, productivity and job creation," Paris 1998.

10. October 7, 1999.

11. Quinn, Brian *et al. Innovation explosion: using intellect and software to revolutionize growth strategies*, The Free Press, New York 1997.

12. Christensen, Clayton. *The Innovator's Dilemma: When great technologies cause great firms to fail*, Harvard Business School Press, Boston, MA 1997.

13. Pieper, Roel. "E-wereld, de ingredienten van de netwerkmaatschappij," October 2000.

14. Smith, K. *et al.* "The Norwegian innovation system: A pilot study of knowledge creation," *STEP Report*, Oslo 1996.

15. Ridder, de W.J. "Concurreren in de kenniseconomie, nieuwe spelers en nieuwe regels," Stichting Maatschappij en Onderneming, Den Haag, February 2001.

16. Douma, Marc *et al.* "Strategic alliances: managing the dynamics of fit," *Long Range Planning*, August 2000.

17. **www.cellular.co.za/gsmhistory.htm**

two

[from internet revolution to
internet evolution]

HOW MANY COMPANIES DO YOU KNOW THAT DIDN'T HAVE AN internet strategy and which got into difficulties? Can you think of any internet applications in your daily life other than e-mail that have fully changed your life?

The internet was brought to us with laser shows and smoke machines. The internet would make the world a better place. It almost sounded like all things negative would be turned into positives by its arrival. There was no longer a place for established companies, which would be made obsolete by start-ups.

The internet revolution has passed though and as the laser shows are over and the last smoke leaves the smoke machines real life goes on. While cleaning up the mess left behind by the internet revolution it becomes clear again that it takes time for a disruptive technology to become part of daily life. Partly because it's hard to build sustainable

As the internet turning into the established entering webs of become dot corps venturing, capital, and revolution **is**

internet evolution,

companies are

innovation **to**

via internal

corporate venture

acquisitions.

and profitable businesses and partly because people are reluctant to change. E-mail was invented in 1972 but it was only extensively adopted in 1999/2000 and beyond. It takes time for something new to become business as usual, after revolution comes evolution.

During the revolution small companies take the lead. In the evolution stage, established players take over where the pioneers left off. Established companies missed out on the first wave but they don't want to miss out on the next one as they don't want to become dinosaurs. While the start-ups that were supposed to make these established companies become obsolete are struggling to survive these established companies are striking back via networked innovation. Based on past experience, they are increasingly acknowledging the importance of being part of webs of innovation to catch the next wave. As the internet revolution is turning into the internet evolution, established companies are entering webs of innovation to become dot corps via internal venturing, corporate venture capital, and acquisitions. Subsequent chapters discuss these issues in more detail. This chapter provides a brief summary of the internet hype and how established companies are striking back as we move from the internet revolution to the internet evolution.

The hype

At the end of 1999 *The Internet Bubble* by the Perkins brothers, founding editors of the Red Herring, was published. In the book they warned of the overvaluation of internet stocks, which in their opinion, symbolizes the madness in that industry. Take for instance eBay, the online auction. On June 1, 1999, the company was valued at $22 billion, 472 times its 1998 revenues. Another example is portal Yahoo – at the same time this company was valued at $30.2 billion. Even though the sales of Yahoo were 90 times smaller it was valued at more than a third of computer manufacturer Dell's valuation.[1]

Interestingly enough this overvaluation is not happening for the first time. In 1968 a number of high tech companies were as hot on Wall Street as some dot coms were at the time the Perkins brothers wrote their book. Two years later their stocks crashed by around 90 percent as shown in Table 2.1. The situation is similar to what has taken place in the past few years.

TABLE 2.1 Hot technology stocks on Wall Street in 1968

Company	1968 high ($)	1970 low ($)	Percentage drop (%)
Fairchild Camera	102	18	−82
Teledyne	72	13	−82
Control Data	163	28	−83
Mohawk Data	111	18	−84
Electronic Data	162	24	−85
Optical Scanning	146	16	−89
Itek	172	17	−90
University Computing	186	13	−93

Source: **www.itulip.com/compare.htm**

In the midst of the hype the larger the loss the better it seemed. "If you're making a profit you're doing something wrong" I once heard one of the "new" economy gurus stating. Small start-ups could easily make established companies become dinosaurs. First you capture market share at all costs and then the next step is to cash in on the market leadership by taking the company public. Then decide what you actually want to do. All of that in a short period, which led to high expectations that were expressed in the outrageous stock prices.

In the early years of the internet, business people were driven by an idealistic desire to change the world. Something new had arrived that was going to change the world. As the first internet companies floated and made their founders very rich, this started to attract people who also wanted a piece of the pie. In 1999 the industry was full of people driven by greed rather than by a passion for the internet industry combined with a thorough understanding of it. As we will find out later in this chapter this is the first sign that the end of a hype is near if everybody wants to be involved.

It seemed as though everybody who started a video store in the eighties was starting a dot com. Just pick a word in the dictionary, add "dot com" then come up with a slick PowerPoint presentation, raise a lot of money and bring your company public and cash in. The majority of these people are going back to the multinationals, consulting or banking or whatever background they came from. The tourists have gone.

People were for instance starting marketplaces for industries they had no expertise or network in. The pitch with these business to business (B2B) companies was that by leveraging the higher speed and efficiency offered by the internet they could help companies do things faster, better, and cheaper. Given the volume of inter-business transactions this would be a perfect market. Venture capital companies were often given the pitch "This is a multibillion market, if we only could have a small stake of that…" As large companies were used to working with electronic data interchange (EDI) it would make the step towards transactions via the internet a smaller one.

In practice, many of these business-to-business (B2B) companies were having a hard time as they found out that people are reluctant to change and that quite often the role of personal relationships is very important. At the end of the day it is the business that drives the technology and not the reverse. Another aspect that contributed to the failure of B2B start-ups was the fact that many established companies were liaising on starting their own exchanges together. Unilever, Cadbury Schweppes, Procter & Gamble, and about 46 other companies joined forces in Transora.com. However, this is not widely viewed as a sustainable business, as the volumes of trading achieved at those exchanges are far from impressive they will probably not obtain follow-up financing from the companies that founded them.

Meanwhile, established companies are building their own online exchanges or private marketplaces to connect with their buyers and suppliers that seem to be far more successful. For example, Covisint, the electronic marketplace founded by the majority of the large car manufacturers such as General Motors and Ford, has so far traded in $350 million in products. Compare this with Volkswagen's own exchange that claims to have traded in products for $930 million.[2] And the start-ups? They changed their business model. They gave up on becoming trading "hubs" and are instead selling the software they developed to established companies that are setting up their own exchanges or to exchanges of alliances. The much-hyped exchange VerticalNet for instance is now selling the software it developed.[3] Rather than changing the structure of industries, these B2B companies reduced transaction costs just as e-mail replaced faxes.[4]

Also interesting were companies that took an old economy business and used the internet instead of a traditional medium. When there was no added value of the internet as channel, when it didn't empower the customer to do something he or she couldn't do before, these companies had a hard time. The online banks are used to illustrate this later in the chapter.

In Europe a lot of American dot com models were copied. Ricardo in Germany and QXL in the UK, for example copied the eBay model. Some of these companies were acquired by their American counterparts as they wanted to enter the European market or quickly grow their market share. Amazon for instance acquired Bookpages in the UK.

Soon enough it became clear again that at the end of the day it's about good execution and access to the right network. Many of the dot coms which fail to realize this become "dot gones," and die. As the times are getting tougher ideas about the route from having an idea to going public are becoming more realistic. It takes time to build a profitable and sustainable business.

The Perkins brothers use the example of the car industry in the US. At the beginning of the 20th century there were about 500 car manufacturers. In 2001 you can count them on one hand after a shake-out and consolidation took place. The situation would be the same for dot coms, predicted the Perkins in their book; a few will succeed in creating a profitable and sustainable organization in about 10–20 years and all the others die or will be acquired. And the stock price of these winners? It won't differ that much of the stock price in 1999 as you will find out later in this chapter.

The arrival of the internet started with a hype leading to a severe overvaluation of dot coms. This overvaluation occurred because the idea was there that these start-ups would make established companies become obsolete and create enormous value. Profit didn't matter, it was all about growing fast, taking the company public and then cashing in. That attracted a lot of greedy and incompetent people. This is changing, however. Since March/April 2000 a shake-out has been taking place, combined with consolidation. Meanwhile established companies are striking back and preparing for the internet evolution by entering webs of innovation to become dot corps. Let's first have a look at life after the hype before we get into how established companies are striking back.

Reality bites

In March 2000, research by the high-profile financial publication *Barron's* predicted that at least 51 dot companies, a quarter of the total, would run out of cash within a year. Previously "buzzed" companies like Cdnow (acquired by Bertelsmann) and Peapod (acquired by Ahold) fall into this category.

The publication by Barron's had its impact on the Nasdaq. After the publication the Nasdaq Composite Index went down by 5 percent. But that drop was just the start. The stock prices continued dropping towards a more realistic valuation. In the third week of April things really moved as the Nasdaq fell 25 percent.

Keep in mind that a few months before this March/April correction 371 stock exchange quoted dot coms together were valued at $1300 billion, comprising around 8 percent of the total value of the stock exchange valuation in the US.[5]

Started by the 1995 flotation of browser producer Netscape and the 1997 flotation of online bookstore Amazon.com the initial public offering (IPO) craze took off. Especially when in September 1998 online auction site eBay floated. On its first day of listing the shares more than doubled. Also of help was an investment banking analyst, Henry Blodget, who forecast that Amazon's shares would break through $400. At that time the shares were still at $240 but his prediction came true in the same month. From then on the number of IPOs kept on increasing. In May 1999 alone 35 internet companies floated in the US.[6] Blodget became a hero and was called "King Henry" in several publications.

Usually it takes

build such a

in this case

lining up

have the

grow at

5–10 years to company. **But investors were to invest** and company internet speed.

Webvan, the American online grocer, had just been around for three months when it floated. Internet service provider Freeserve, and Lastminute.com kick-started the IPO craze in Europe. Worldwide, television coverage showed people in Hong Kong standing in lines for hours to sign up for the flotation of Tom.com, the portal of the well-known Hong Kong entrepreneur Richard Li. The IPO craze was in full motion on a global basis.

Soon after the US a similar correction followed in Europe with the crash of World Online after its IPO. The flotation of this internet service provider was expected to become a huge success. In practice the shares crashed. Floated at a price per share of €43 in March 2000 the price was around €14 by the beginning of April.

At Nasdaq the stock of 90 percent of dot coms was trading below the offer price in January 2001 and 100 dot coms had stock prices below the $1 threshold needed to maintain a listing.[7]

Consider once more Table 2.1 and then look at Table 2.2, showing hot dot com stocks during and after the hype, and reach your own conclusions.

In his book on hypes *Devil take the hindmost* Edward Chancellor reasons that the majority of these stocks will go down in value by at least another 50 percent. The reasoning behind this is that the return on capital over time is usually about 7.5 percent. That makes a price/earnings multiple of about 15 instead of the 30 price/earnings multiple we see now. So be prepared, the valuations are still too high and a second correction might follow.

For companies in the new economy the "old economy" standards apply again. That is why a number of companies have postponed their IPO. Good companies still deserve good valuations though. Examples of good IPOs in Europe were Egg (an internet bank) and Telia (Swedish

TABLE 2.2 Hot dot com stocks during the hype in 2000 in Europe

Company	2000 high	2000 low	Percentage drop
QXL Ricardo	800p	6.5p	−99
Musicmusicmusic	11.8	1.25	−89
Lastminute.com	562.5p	64.5p	−89
Scoot	357p	59p	−84
T-Online	48	12.19	−75
Freeserve	977.5p	90p	−91
Lycos Europe N.V.	23.3	3.6	−85

Source: Wall Street Journal Europe, January 8 2001. All prices in euros, except where noted with p for pence.

Telco). The stock prices of these companies did not increase 200–300 percent after their IPO but stayed around their introduction price.

At an event with a lot of "movers and shakers" from the industry in London, a speaker delivered an interesting key note with the title "Who should go to jail?" In other words whose fault is the IPO craze? Take for instance Letsbuyit.com. The idea behind the company was that consumers would get discounts on products by buying them as a group. An unproven, new and very complex business model. Usually it takes 5–10 years to build such a company. But in this case investors were lining up to invest and have the company grow at internet speed. Well-known European venture capitalists such as Gilde and Nesbic had backed the company. It was taken public by FleetBoston Robertson Stephens (lead) in July 2000 and floated at €3.5 but was at €0.27 at the end of January 2001 when it was about to go bankrupt and struggling to survive. Investors were no longer interested. At that time the company had about

320 employees in several European countries. The company had grown far too fast. So who should go to jail? There are a number of contenders:

- Managers for mismanagement?

- The investment banks that wanted to raise as much money as possible and therefore made the valuation of the companies they took public as high as possible as their fee is a percentage of the valuation of the placement?

- The journalists for over-sensationalizing instead of providing a thorough and rational analysis?

- Day traders who acted too impulsively?

- The venture capitalists who wanted a quick exit at a high valuation?

Probably everybody was equally guilty. This is an example of what psychologists call "group think."

Follow the crowd

The arrival of the internet united a huge group of people and created the shared feeling that the world would become a better place. Deep inside people are driven to join a majority with a unanimity in thinking. "Group think" allows individuals to substitute agreement for analysis. The group tends to exclude everything that "does not fit their picture," including negative consequences or risks as they are ignored or glossed over. Things can't go wrong and those that disagree haven't understood it. It seems as though that was what happened to us. That way everybody is equally guilty. We should *all* go to jail. And Letsbuyit.com? The company was lucky and ended up finding financing but lots of companies in similar circumstances died.

Where to next?

Things have gotten back to normal though and dot coms get the same rational analysis as all "old" economy companies that decide to go public. There are no longer huge differences between the flotation of "old" economy companies and "new" economy companies. Investors have woken up from the dream of the hype and are getting back to business basics – investing in healthy companies with realistic revenues and profits. These companies take time to grow. Not one or two years but five to ten years. This applies equally to the "new" economy as it does to the "old" economy. It is not as easy as investing a lot in order to build a huge customer base, go IPO and done. It is hard and takes time to build a profitable and sustainable business. Although incubators make you think this is a process you can standardize, that is not the case. It is an organic process that you cannot artificially accelerate, no matter how many people you employ or how much funding you have.

However, who knows what other craze the future will bring? Crazes are not unique to the last two centuries. Hypes have been around for ages. Take for instance the tulip mania in the 17th century in Europe.

These days the tulip flower is one of the trademarks of Holland. You can buy a bag of tulip bulbs for a few dollars. Would you believe that there was a time that people bought one single tulip bulb for a couple of hundreds of dollars? As a matter of fact there was such a time, during the "tulip mania" of the 17th century. For example, one type – called Viceroy – sold for around $350 at the height of its popularity. Evidence has been found showing that even houses, businesses, or ships were traded for a single tulip bulb. Tulip prices were listed in newspapers just as stocks are these days. People left their occupations to trade in or grow tulip bulbs, people borrowed money and took extra mortgages to be able to do this. Initially the trading took place in

The market wedding rings downloading was not going to sustain competing

for buying online **or best man jokes** to be big enough half a dozen **companies.**

taverns in the Netherlands but soon the craze spread to other European countries. The hype ended in 1637, when the Dutch government came up with legislation stating that tulip bulbs could not be investments and that they could only be paid for in cash and therefore loans could no longer be issued by banks with tulips as its collateral. A chain reaction followed resulting in thousands of people going bankrupt. Replace "tulip-bulb" with "dot com" and the Dutch government in 1637 with the Barron's report and you see a surprising number of similarities. The pattern seems to be same – something new comes up while the economy is doing well, group think develops as something new arrives, everybody wants to be involved, and suddenly the hype is stopped leaving behind a mess which leads to a temporary economic downturn to recover from the hype.

After all the hypes, there should be a feeling of "we will never let a hype happen to us again" but unfortunately it is always overruled by greed when new hypes emerge. It will be interesting to see what the next hype will be. Would you be able to resist the greed?

As we're cleaning up the mess left behind after the hype things are getting back to normal. Those start-ups that had planned an IPO to raise money to compensate the losses for the coming years will be disappointed as old economy criteria will also be applied to new economy criteria before floating. You can't float a concept. Besides that, venture capital companies are far more demanding these days since the "exit" via an IPO takes more time and is less obvious. Companies without revenues and too high monthly costs might face the same fate as Boo.com. This high-profile online clothes retailer backed by well-known organizations such as Benetton and people such as Bernard Arnault, chairman of Louis Vuitton Moet Hennessy, had a burn-rate of $130 million in six months. The VCs no longer found it attractive to invest in this company and in May 2000 the company declared itself bankrupt and the technology was sold for $372,000 (Boo had developed it for $50 million) to Bright Station, while the brand and domain name were sold for an unknown amount to Fashionmall.[8]

Other companies that were initially hyped and later followed the same pattern as Boo.com are Craftshop.com, DEN, NetImperative, RedRocket.com, Toysmart.com, Violet.com, and WebGalaxy. The suffering dot coms are also an easy buy for established companies. This is discussed in greater detail in Chapter 5.

In the struggle to survive, consolidation is an alternative to being acquired. In September 2000 for instance all the main wedding portals in the UK joined forces. They found out that combined, they would be stronger than as separate entities, especially as many of them were offering complementary products. The market for buying wedding rings online or downloading best man jokes was not going to be big enough to sustain half a dozen competing companies.[9] Consolidation made them stronger as a whole.

Besides joining forces with other companies or being acquired many companies stayed independent and tried to reinvent their business. The dynamics around finding the right business model lead to interesting moves. A trend is that dot coms license the technology around their business. As I described earlier, that is something done by B2B companies but it is also done by business-to-consumer (B2C) companies.

Amazon licensed one of its core technologies, the patented 1-Click system which saves information on customers so they do not have to fill out all information with every purchase), to Apple. Also eBay (one of the few companies that quickly made it into the black) announced by the end of September 2000 that it would license its auction software.[10]

Now the romance is over for these companies it becomes increasingly clear that customer acquisition and retention is hard. It's not without reason that it takes a while to build a good company in the B2C space.

Winners in the internet revolution

So far in the consumer market a few large players have stood out, such as Amazon and Yahoo. Amazon for instance has 25 million paying customers and is expected to have sold about $2.5 billion worth of books, electronics, and kitchen gadgets in 2000.[11] The company is still not in the black but has created a strong brand and still has significant funds in the bank.

It is still not clear whether they have a sustainable business model. Let's have a look at the other large player, Yahoo. Perceived by many as one of the winners of the internet revolution, in March 2000 this company's valuation was more than the combined valuation of Boeing, HJ Heinz, and General Motors.[12] The question remains whether the company will also be a winner in the internet evolution. The company's revenues are mostly based on advertising. As the online advertisements interest and rates are declining Yahoo has to find alternative ways of income. It has begun to charge for some of its services and is developing new services such as developing internal websites for large companies. It has launched a B2B marketplace and offers companies a service where they can pay to be showed on top with search queries. If the company does not succeed in finding alternative revenue streams it will fail, to be replaced perhaps by a new player with a better revenue model. In March 2001 key executives left the company and the company was down from a peak valuation of $115 billion in 2000 to $9.7 billion in early March 2001. Rumours were rife that Yahoo was looking for a company to acquire it.

But Yahoo is still doing relatively well. The company still serves millions of customers everyday with good services under a very valuable brand name. So far the company has been profitable and has a huge pile of cash in the bank. Many other consumer market companies have a hard time finding a sustainable and profitable business model. In the next ten years it might turn out that a lot of these consumer market companies were great but were on the scene too early. If you look at the statistics of online retail you can see how early the stage is we're in now. The US Census Bureau found that in 1999 about half a percent of all retail sales took place on the Internet.[13] In the future it might be some new players reinventing ideas of the past but with customers who are ready for it.

The costs of some of these B2C dot coms were impressive, especially in retail. High profile online store Webvan lost in the fourth quarter of 1999 about $13 per order. Toystore eToys lost about $4 per order and sports store Fogdog about $5.[14] In particular costs for aftersales customer care and databases turned out to be higher than expected. B2C companies are far from where they could be.

Imagine yourself walking around a supermarket and you see empty shopping carts all around you. Furthermore you see some confused people walking around because they can't find the cashier. This scenario is probably hard to imagine. On the internet, this is common – according to the Boston Consulting Group[15] about 69 percent of the visitors to internet shops do not finalize their purchase. Especially with the competitor one click away this is dangerous. Among investors a shared believe seemed to be created that you shouldn't invest in B2C companies as they can't make money. I think that the only problem is that they are in an early stage and still have a lot to work out, which takes time. However, good companies will definitely arrive in this space.

Meanwhile these B2C companies have developed a very valuable asset, their technology. Especially now that all large companies want to become dot corps an interesting customer group comes into existence. It seems as though things are changing from dot coms taking on the established companies to make them become obsolete towards dot coms working together with established companies helping them become dot corps. Examples are not only less well-known companies like Homebid.com but also better-known companies such as eBay. They are all in search of things that increase revenue streams and are finding out that established companies can provide avenues to achieve this.

One of the first companies to have discovered this is CNET. This company spun off a company in 1996 that sells its publication software, Vignette. The company floated in 1999. In September 2000 this company was valued at $6.25 billion.[16]

Cost-cutting moves – advertising and HR

A less creative way of getting into the black is to reduce costs. With dot coms the first things to go are often advertising and human resources.

The idea with advertising during the hype seemed to be that the more you advertise the more you sell. Sometimes it seemed as though buzz was confused with business plan. Figure 2.1 shows how much these companies spent on advertising compared to their sales revenues.

As dot coms matured, their spending on advertising did as well. The mantra "the more you advertise, the more you sell" wasn't hip anymore. Still, whereas Amazon, America Online, and Wit Capital are seen as the "new" economy darlings they still spend far more than "old" economy advertising big spender Procter & Gamble.

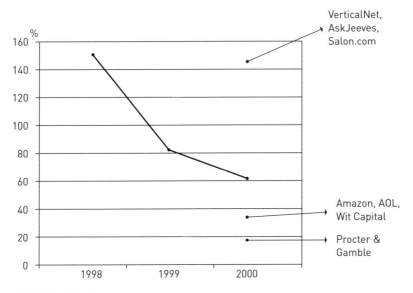

FIGURE 2.1 Dot com advertising madness

Source: freedgar.com, thestandard .com

Another way to cut costs was through human resources. The recruiting pattern with a lot of dot coms was very wild. When things seemed to be going well, recruitment was high. When things were going less well, they were made redundant. With the management fully focused on assuring new rounds of financing and securing the first customers, human resources was not always the first priority – and could in some cases be a mess as human resources were not efficiently used. Sometimes that could lead to funny situations. The best illustration of this was a journalist for *The New Yorker* who walked into an office of a New York city based dot com and managed to fake being an employee for three weeks.

However, as things got serious again this was over. At the end of 2000 a lot of members of the dot com workforce spent their Christmas unemployed as companies were trying to cut costs via layoffs.

In New York's equivalent of Silicon Valley, Silicon Alley, monthly gatherings are organized for people that were made redundant at start-ups – "pink-slip parties." The name derived from American redundancy forms. These parties have hundreds of attendees. After a wild ride in a dot com, the majority of the pink-slip attendees would like to join a more established company that wants to become a dot corp.[17] Many of this "new economy workforce" were disappointed by their experiences with start-ups. During the hype it seemed as though a sort of idealized view of working for a start-up had been created – informal and without stress. Start-ups turned out to have their darker sides as well.

The enormous drive of all employees in a start-up to succeed and to become part of the establishment comes at a price. Stress and tensions are the result. Working for a dot corp seems to be an attractive alternative. With the plunging of the stock prices, cost cutting, and shakeouts, many former dot com employees are finding the best of both worlds in e-ventures of established companies, separate companies set up for the internet activities of the parent. There is stability because of the availability of enough capital, the backing by a well-known brand, expertise and an impressive customer and partners base on one hand and the freedom of a start-up on the other hand. To established companies these employees bring start-up expertise, which is a new area for a lot of these companies.

What has been learned?

By finding new revenue streams and cutting down costs, dot coms are discovering that the internet revolution did not change one fundamental business rule – if you want to make a profit, your revenues have to be higher than your costs. Many dot coms are experiencing that. Even companies that had a "first movers" glamour around them have to prove themselves. It might be great to have a lot

By finding new revenue streams and **cutting down costs**, dot coms are discovering that the internet revolution **did not change one fundamental business rule** – if you want to make a **profit**, your **revenues** have to be **higher** than your **costs**.

of buzz around a company but at the end of the day, it's about making a profit and building a sustainable business. In the internet evolution it's not about first movers anymore but about first *provers*. Table 2.3 contains some examples of companies that were first movers but which failed to become first provers.

TABLE 2.3 First movers that did not become first provers

Company name	What they offered
Boo.com	Clothes store
Boxman	Music store
Clickmango.com	Health advisory site
Etoys	Online toys store
Living.com	Furniture
Mothernature.com	Health store
Pets.com	Pets store
Pseudo Programs	Movie producer
Streamline.com	Store delivery

Note: not all were "first movers" but all were seen as "high profile" leading companies.

A group that played a significant role during the hype are the venture capitalists (VCs). Over the past few years some Silicon Valley VCs reached a star status. Some of them, such as Ann Winnblad of Hummer Winnblad, were perceived as the preachers of the "new" economy evangelism and were frequently quoted in the media discussing many interesting things besides what it is all about – performance of their funds.

With the advent of the "new" economy, venture capital financing was sexy again. It brought a lot of money into your company enabling you to grab as much land as possible to benefit from first mover advantages, take your company public, meaning that there was enough money to reorganize your business and consider the "minor issue" of how to make money. Meanwhile your investors sold out and then went through the whole process again.

In practice, things go slower than you think and doing something too fast can lead to chaos. There will be many "behind the scenes" stories in the media in coming years – reported, no doubt, by the same journalists who first helped to create the hype.

Dot coms found that even though an idea is simple, building a good company takes time. Coming up with a good idea happens relatively easily, building a company takes time. Having a lot of money from a venture capital company doesn't change that.

An interesting outcome in the book *The origin and evolution of new businesses* by Professor Amar Bhide of Columbia University is the fact that the majority of successful companies are "accidental companies." For example, Pierre Omidyar founded eBay to help his wife collect Pez candy dispensers. It just happened. A minority of the researched start-ups had written a detailed business plan. The majority of these companies were started with an average capital of $10,000. Cisco, producer of routers (the traffic agents of the internet), for instance was started with money from the founders themselves and without a thorough business plan. It was only in the so-called second round of financing that VCs joined in. Nowadays the majority of internet traffic passes through Cisco routers.

This is altogether a different story from what VCs generally consider to be the secret to successful ventures, i.e. experienced founders, thorough market analysis, detailed business plan, top-notch management team (MBAs, experience with top strategic consultants/investment bank/multinational), and sufficient financing. Many companies matching this profile are experiencing severe problems. That brings us back to the VCs. Once the heroes of the "new" economy, they are also now suffering as the hype is over.

At InsiderVC.com you can find information on performance of American funds. InsiderVC.com founder and editor Stephen Lisson collected investment information sent out by funds to potential limited partners (investors in VC funds) and other sources for years. This forms a very interesting database. With regard to return on investment, VCs tend to be vague and are not afraid of "window dressing," making things look better than they are. Take for instance Hummer Winnblad. This fund used to be a "sexy" VC in the Valley. One of the founders, Ann Winnblad, was often to be heard speaking at conferences or in interviews with the media telling us where the world was going. On InsiderVC.com you can read that the 1997 fund of Hummer Winnblad has so far returned only 42 percent of its investors' money. This might seem to be a fair return but it is important to remember that other funds active at the same time brought in similar profits. For example, Kleiner Perkins Caufield & Byers already made 1000 percent profit for its 1996 fund.[18] At the end of the day that's what venture capital is about – delivering an attractive return on investment (ROI) for the

The railroads, electricity **have much more** changes than

telegraph and brought about dramatic the internet has so far.

limited partners (investors in the fund). Don't be surprised to see a shake-out among VCs in the coming years as it becomes apparent that some funds have significantly underperformed.

Whereas during the hype everything was cool as long as it had ".com" after it, turning an idea into a sustainable and profitable business is hard. Reality bites. This leads to a shake-out as companies struggle to survive. As discussed earlier in this chapter, costs are often reduced by spending less on advertising and making employees redundant. Creative new revenue streams such as licensing the technology are found. Being acquired or joining forces with similar companies is another survival strategy. Established companies seemed to be absent from the internet revolution. The internet revolution was supposed to make them obsolete but the opposite seems to be happening. Start-ups and established companies are joining forces to help established companies become dot corps. This is examined in greater detail later in this chapter.

The good news is that the development of the internet is just beginning as the hype, driven by a herd-like behavior has passed. We're just at the beginning of the internet wave and probably have no idea of all of great things the internet is going to bring us during the internet evolution.

It's just starting

It's "scene I, act II", a phrase you often hear in relation to the internet. Everybody is just starting to understand the internet. If you look at many of the major disruptive technologies in history you will see that there has always been a long time between the introduction of a disruptive technology and its becoming mature and accepted. Change takes time.

In the western world it took about 500 years before the majority of the population could write and there are a significant number of illiterate people still. Although printing was a 15th-century innovation, the first weekly newspaper appeared in 1609. Between the invention of electricity and its usage by the majority of industries, there was a 40-year lapse. It takes time for something to become mature and accepted. Table 2.4 shows some of the major disruptive technologies of the past centuries.

TABLE 2.4 Major disruptive technologies

Micro-electronics	Steel
Software	Electric power
Digital networks	Chemicals
Internet	Internal combustion engine
Printing	Telephone
Water power	Petrochemicals
Textiles	Electronics
Iron	Air travel
Steam	New media
Railroads	Television

The internet appears to be following the same pattern. The railroads, telegraph, and electricity have brought about much more dramatic changes than the internet has so far. Electric light extended the working day, and railroads allowed goods and people to be moved much more quickly and easily across the country.[19] How does the internet fit in here? What changes has it brought so far?

We're just at the beginning of the internet wave. As well as the innovations that still need to take place, the acceptance of this disruptive technology also takes time. Although PCs are already entering the mass market, the internet is still in its infancy.

A marketing classic with the adoption of new technologies is the S-curve. Basically this theory states that the penetration of the market by a new technology over time occurs via an S-shaped curve. The PC is further in terms of penetration than the internet (see Figure 2.2). This is supported by research by the Organization for Economic Co-operation and Development (OECD) that clearly shows that the global penetration of the PC is higher than that of the Internet.[20] The question is what needs to happen to make this penetration rise?

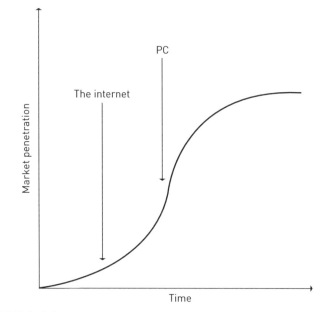

FIGURE 2.2 The internet is just starting to reach the masses

When did you get your first business e-mail account? Although you probably couldn't live without it these days it's not too long ago that companies first started to use the internet. We're slowly reaching the stage where usage of the internet is maturing as companies discover for instance that the internet can establish significant savings on purchases and so on. It seems to be moving from using the internet as a marketing tool – somewhere to put your brochure on – towards the internet being a key part of the main business.

Inventor of the world wide web, Tim Berners-Lee, stated it pretty well in an interview with new economy magazine *Business 2.0*: "Having been completely unaware of the web, companies rushed into it for the sake of it – which was the wrong point of view. Now companies are going about their proper business, selling tyres or whatever it is and the web is just part of their machinery, just as the phone system and pencil are. Everybody is getting more used to accepting the web as part of life. So I think the excitement of being on the web for its own sake is disappearing and the web's getting more mature."[21]

An interesting case is the English railroad boom in the 1830s. The boom led to a shake-out in the beginning of the 1840s. Once this had happened, the industry really took off and companies were building railroads and making a profit by doing that.[22] You can see a similar pattern with the internet. A boom between 1995 and 2000 and a serious start afterwards. I met with a lot of experts and while opinions varied, it is likely that during the next ten years, the internet will bring us things that will change our lives. So it's just starting. I'm sure we have no idea of how things are going to change and that we've only seen the tip of the iceberg. It will take time before we know what changes the internet has brought us and we will probably laugh at the current situation. Consider the history of the windshield wiper for example. The first automobiles had no windshield and if it rained you just got wet. Then the windshield were invented and people enjoyed staying dry but visibility was still poor when it rained. It was Gladstone Adams who came up with the idea of working out a device to scrape the windshield clean. Nowadays you would laugh at the idea of driving without a windshield and wiper blades. Evolution takes time. Figure 2.3 suggests a likely development curve for the internet.

Highly complex ideas were considered in relation to the internet, such as buying with groups, exchanges, etc. So far not too many entirely new business models have been created. It turned out that its simplest applications are the most successful. Consider e-mail, for example. It has had a huge impact on both professional and private lives. In 2000, 1.47 billion e-mail messages a day were sent.[23] E-mail made communication faster and easier. The world wide web and browser combination had a similar effect. It enabled easier access to information that wasn't possible before. This was the first step in changing the internet from an exclusive communications network for academics to a

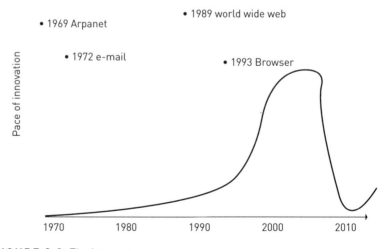

FIGURE 2.3 The internet wave

global communications network for the masses allowing them to interact, conduct transactions, and to access information.

The internet is crossing the chasm as guru Geoff Moore would state. From the early guys to the mainstream market. From nerds to the guy next door. Even now only about 5 percent of the global population has access to the internet. But to what extent did it drastically change the way these people relate to each other and do business? Think of your own situation. How did the internet change your life? I use Hotmail, instant messaging, have websites and backup my files on the internet via Freedrive but that's it. Even then I still consider myself a bit of an early adopter. People are resistant to change, so it takes time to change people and that has been one of the things underestimated during the hype. You can't accelerate the acceptance of change by people, no matter how much money you have.

The internet was hailed as an interactive medium that would enrich our lives. So far the only thing offered by the internet is information. But even that is chaotic. As the majority access the internet via analog telephone lines not too much can be done as the telephone lines put a limit on the amount of data that can be downloaded. Many web pages take too long to download as they are often designed by people who presume that everybody is already using broadband access. Many of the pages are dull and are not user friendly. However, many state that the current state of the internet could be compared to the silent movie era of cinema, awaiting color, sound, and special effects.[24] The next ten years will bring much more.

In the first act there was a euphoric atmosphere where the mantra was that small start-ups would make established companies obsolete but in the second act things are settling in and the established companies prepared in silence to strike back. In the second act it's no longer a question of start-ups trying to make established companies become obsolete or the reverse but about start-ups that work *with* established companies to enable them to become dot corps. There might be a few new large players emerging that take on existing players but that will be a minority. The majority of the start-ups will help established companies become dot corps.

As with all other previous disruptive technologies, a lot of players are trying to build a profitable and sustainable business out of the internet. After a shake-out and consolidation, only a few key players will remain. The established companies are still there. They missed out on the internet revolution but seem eager to come back in the internet evolution. Subsequent chapters show how they're doing that via networked innovation but let us first consider how the established companies are doing now the internet revolution is over.

As with all other previous **disruptive technologies**, a lot of players are **trying to build** a profitable and **sustainable business** out of the internet. After a shake-out and consolidation, **only a few key players will remain.**

Established companies striking back

The Christmas lesson

Christmas 1999 was supposed to be a showcase for how online web stores would make established companies obsolete. It was heralded as a Christmas that would make its mark in internet history. It did make its mark but unfortunately for online web stores, it was not a positive one. Orders were delivered too late, incomplete, wrong or – even worse – not at all. Overall, it proved to something of a slap in the face for online web stores. So what went wrong?

Logistics proved to be more difficult than expected. Making sure every customer gets what he or she ordered, on time and in good condition is hard. It is also difficult to ensure that the customer is satisfied – and stays that way. And then I haven't even mentioned doing this in a profitable way.

By Christmas 2000, these companies had learned their lesson but nevertheless an interesting thing occurred. The supposed to be dinosaurs – established companies – were striking back online. Eight of the fastest growing US retail sites, in terms of traffic volume, for the peak-selling week ending December 10, 2000 were online ventures of established companies such as Wal-Mart.com, Nordstrom.com, and Bluelight (Kmart).[25] Once again a slap in the face of the "pure play" online web stores. It would appear that it's not so easy to make these established companies obsolete.

Some examples

E-businesses are most likely to succeed when they are most like those that worked *before* the internet. Consider the case of banking via the internet. During the hype, internet banks were seen as the big new thing. They would make the established banks obsolete. In practice, it turned out that the internet as a single medium was not sufficient for banking. It became more successful as part of the offering of established banks. Pure play internet banks therefore began to broaden their range of offerings, adding services that were already offered by established banks.

E*Trade, for example, purchased 8500 ATM machines in March 2000. E*Trade also plans to open financial services kiosks in stores of supermarket giant Target. That way Target customers can carry out brokerage and banking transactions in the store, use an E*Trade-branded ATM, and speak with an on-site E*Trade representative.[26] Customers still seem reluctant to be with a bank without a physical presence. Although the internet changes businesses and people's daily lives, the way people relate to each other remains the same, just as it remained the same with other disruptive technologies such as aviation, electricity, and railroads. They made life easier but didn't change how people relate to each other.

US pharmacy chain Walgreens has a website on which prescriptions can be ordered online. As opposed to the "everything will be online and everything off-line will become obsolete" way of thinking, the website did not harm the stores in anyway. On the contrary, about 90 percent of customers placing orders via the website prefer to pick up their prescriptions at the pharmacy.[27] Instead of making the business obsolete, the internet *improved* the business. For many established companies, the internet is a new channel that perfectly complements existing channels. For these companies it is not a case of doing something online or failing but of providing a welcome addition to their existing channels.

The established companies have benefited internally from the internet by significant cost savings, either with how companies run their business internally or by the way companies interact with buyers and suppliers. By making standard purchases or having employees fill out expense claims via the internet, established companies make impressive savings.

Cisco often claims to do the majority of its business via the internet and is saving hundreds of millions of dollars by using the internet, extranet or their intranet for a variety of functions, including expense claims and recruitment. In addition, changes in the supply chain lead to significant savings. Established companies are setting up their private marketplaces to make procurement more efficient as I described earlier in this chapter. Airlines are increasingly selling tickets via the internet, cutting out expensive intermediaries. Delta Airlines sold 5 percent of its tickets online in 2000, representing $400 million in revenue, but even more importantly, resulting in significant cost reduction. When selling a round trip via a travel agent the cost is $10 and about 70 percent of tickets are sold in this way. Selling a ticket for the same trip via the internet costs almost nothing.[28] However, the same is not true for all companies or industries. Philips for instance has chosen to help its approximately 60,000 resellers online instead of selling to customers directly behind their back. The company learned from Sony, which dropped its plans for direct customer sales after its dealers and distributors protested.[29] However, within businesses in which the internet is nothing more than an extra distribution channel (such as the banking industry), established companies seem to win.

For businesses in which the internet allows customers to do things they could not do before or make them faster, better, or cheaper, established companies are challenged as their industry might be completely changed by new players (either established companies from unrelated industries or start-ups). Dell changed the computer industry by offering customers the opportunity to customize their own

As things are

business as usual

that these

companies have

such as

channels,

brands, and so on

start-ups are

becoming
it turns out
established
a lot to offer,
**distribution
established
– all things which
struggling with.**

PCs online, something they could not do before. It is in businesses like these that webs of innovations are developing that might one day make them become obsolete. Threatened established companies should make sure that they enter these networks via networked innovation to survive the internet evolution and become dot corps.

David and Goliath joining forces

Dot coms were supposed to take over from the established companies. Entire industries would be turned upside down by these start-ups and there would be no room for the established companies. These "Goliaths" seem to have woken up because of all the noise made by the "Davids." The Davids have made the Goliaths aware of the great things the internet is going to bring us. However, the Davids aren't doing too well anymore. How will David and Goliath relate to each other in the internet evolution? Will this time the established companies strike back and make the start-ups obsolete?

Now it seems that the internet revolution is over, in the internet evolution, established players take over. The time that the shared vision was that in the new economy virtual networks of small companies would take over from the established giants has gone. As things are becoming business as usual it turns out that these established companies have a lot to offer, such as distribution channels, established brands, and so on – all things which start-ups are struggling with. Meanwhile established companies are increasingly acknowledging that start-ups are often better at developing immature markets. Instead of fighting each other they are now working together in webs of innovation. Goliaths and Davids working together on the new new thing. Both doing what they're best at. The start-ups in creating new competences and the established companies in expanding them.

In the past, large companies facilitated research and development by financing and doing it themselves but they are now beginning to realize the potential of webs of innovation as gateways to new new things. An increasing number of corporations proactively enter these webs of innovation in an increasingly structured way. Networked innovation seems to have three key components:

- internal venturing

- corporate venture capital

- acquisitions.

Some are trying to enter webs of innovation by starting a separate, often-competitive, e-venture. Procter & Gamble, for instance, started Reflect.com. Wal-Mart formed Wal-Mart.com, and there are many more examples of young, e-ventures from old, more traditional companies.

Another key component is corporate venture capital, of which Intel is a well-known example. In 1991 the company started its venture capital activities. In March 2001 its portfolio was worth $3.3 billion.[30] Although this was a great achievement, of greater importance have been the strategic contributions achieved thanks to its investments. As an example, Intel credits its investments in online B2B technology vendors for helping the company's internal internet people "realize what can be done." The company now generates over $1 billion of sales per month over the web.[31]

The third key component is acquisitions. Grocery giant Ahold, for example, acquired online grocery store Peapod. Media giant Bertelsmann acquired peer-to-peer music exchange Napster and online CD store CDnow. As these companies are often struggling to survive, they are relatively cheap to buy. Established companies can buy the technology, back and front office of the dot com.

Established companies are increasingly structuring for networked innovation. Some of them are even setting up separate structures composed of the three key components of networked innovation (internal venturing, corporate venture capital, and acquisitions) – so-called "networked innovation nodes." However, all of this is in an early stage, there is a great deal of experimentation going on and fine tuning of strategies.

There is no single best way yet for mature old economy companies to enter webs of innovation. However, they are increasingly trying to do so; and how they do it will undoubtedly influence the way companies will look in the information age.

Established companies are striking back.

Conclusion

Although the internet was introduced in a blaze of publicity, it is only the beginning. After the hype in which the sky was the limit, reality bites. After April 2000, it became clear that it is difficult to build profitable and sustainable businesses.

So far we've only seen the tip of the internet iceberg. It's scene I, act II. While start-ups are experiencing a shake-out and consolidation, established companies are regaining ground. As they missed out in the internet revolution, they are making sure they do not miss out in the internet evolution. For some established companies the internet is nothing more than an extra distribution channel, yet for others the internet might turn around their industry. For the latter it means that they should especially make sure to become part of the right webs of innovation. Traumatized by their struggles in the past with innovation in immature markets it seems as though established companies are increasingly structuring their networked innovation activities. All of this to become part of the relevant webs of innovation ensuring they become dot corps. David joining forces with Goliath.

Before discussing how companies are structuring these activities, we will explore the three key components of networked innovation – internal venturing, corporate venture capital, and acquisitions – in the following chapters.

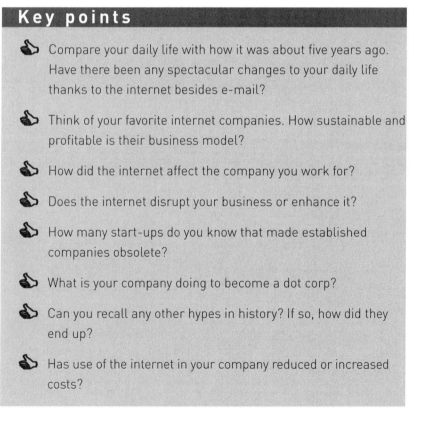

Key points

- 👍 Compare your daily life with how it was about five years ago. Have there been any spectacular changes to your daily life thanks to the internet besides e-mail?

- 👍 Think of your favorite internet companies. How sustainable and profitable is their business model?

- 👍 How did the internet affect the company you work for?

- 👍 Does the internet disrupt your business or enhance it?

- 👍 How many start-ups do you know that made established companies obsolete?

- 👍 What is your company doing to become a dot corp?

- 👍 Can you recall any other hypes in history? If so, how did they end up?

- 👍 Has use of the internet in your company reduced or increased costs?

👉 Think of your favorite established stores. Are they working on an e-strategy?

Further information

At the website **www.websofinnovation.com** you can find additional resources on the subject, such as links to relevant articles, books, websites and over time this will be expanded. A mailing list on the subject of this chapter allows you to discuss it with other readers.

Notes

1. OECD. "OECD Information Technology Outlook," Paris 2000.

2. Grande, Carlos and Hill, Andrew. "Big business gets to grip with net savings," *Financial Times*, London, March 6, 2001.

3. Foremski, Tom and Hill, Andrew. "Software groups join forces as the going gets tougher," *Financial Times*, London, March 7, 2001.

4. Hansell, Saul. "Now that we're still here, where do we go? Seven answers," *New York Times*, New York, NY, February 28, 2001.

5. Loudon, Alexander. "Internet becomes business as usual," *Planet Multimedia*, Amersfoort 2000.

6. OECD. "OECD Information Technology Outlook", Paris 2000.

7. Kim, Chan and Mauborgne, Renee. "How to tell a flyer from a failure," *Financial Times*, London, January 23, 2001.

8. Giussani, Bruno. "Amid turmoil, European net industry begins to reshape," *New York Times*, New York, NY, June 15, 2000.

9. "Only the strong survive after the storm," *Financial Times*, London, October 6, 2000.

10. "NetTrends: Online retailers try selling the store," Internetnews.com, September 2000.

11. Hansell, Saul. "As boldest e-commerce ventures fall, modest dreamers fly on," *New York Times*, NY, December 13, 2000.

12. Slater, Paul. "What a difference a year makes," *Financial Times*, London, March 10, 2001.

13. Hopper, Ian. "Census Bureau releases e-commerce figures," Foxnews.com, March 7, 2001.

14. van Elburg, Anton. "Winnaars gezocht," *Emerce*, December 2000.

15. "Cash in on Christmas." Pp.7–17, *Business 2.0*, UK edition, December 2000.

16. Loudon, Alexander. "From first movers to first provers," *Planet Multimedia*, Amersfoort 2000.

17. Delio, Michelle. "Laid-off dot-commer? Let's party." *Wired*, September 30, 2000.

18. "Behind the VC music," *ValleyTalk*, Fortune.com, November 22, 2000.

19. "Untangling e-conomics," *The Economist*, September 23, 2000.

20. "OECD Information Technology Outlook 2000," Organization for Economic Co-operation and Development, Paris 2000.

21. Wright, Jonathan . "The quiet revolutionary," *Business 2.0*, UK edition, December 2000.

22. Daly, James. "Sage advice," *Business 2.0,* August 8, 2000.

23. Tweney, Dylan. "How to customize customer support," *The Defogger* at **www.ecompany.com/defogger**, March 21, 2001.

24. Leadbeater, Charles. "Dotcoms will rise again," *New Statesman*, January 15, 2001.

25. Kehoe, Louise. "Christmas cheer for off-line brands," *Financial Times*, December 20, 2000.

26. Koller, Lynn. "Web banks in trouble," *Bank Technology News*, September 2000.

27. Porter, Michael. "Strategy and the internet," *Harvard Business Review*, Harvard Business School Publishing, Boston, MA, March 2001.

28. Hammonds, Keith. "Delta's web strategy takes flight," in *Fast Company*, October 2000.

29. Dorsey, James. "Philips to set up online network for its product resellers," *Wall Street Journal Europe*, January 16, 2001.

30. Williams, Molly. "Corporate Venture Capital Cools Off," *Wall Street Journal Europe*, July 5, 2001.

31. Werbach. "How big companies respond," in Release 1.0, EDventure Holdings, New York, NY, January 2000.

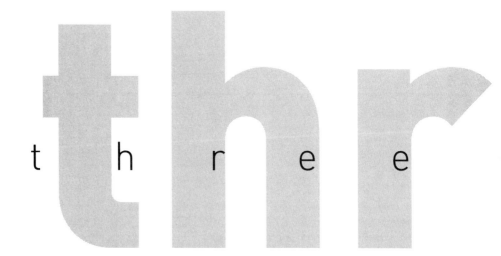

t h r e e

[internal venturing]

IN 1997 A GROUP OF ERICSSON EMPLOYEES LEFT THE COMPANY
to set up a company called Altitun, backed by venture capital and
informal investors. The company's core product, a tuneable laser,
enables flexible bandwidth provisioning, an idea conceived by the
founders while they were employees at Ericsson. In May 2000 the
company was acquired by ADC Telecommunications. Based on ADC's
closing share price of $57.25 on May 4, 2000, the acquisition was
valued at approximately $872 million – pretty good value creation in
about three years. But none of that created value went to Ericsson
although the ideas forming the basis of the company were perceived
there.

The people behind Altitun were not the first to leave Ericsson. The
company had seen a lot of other talented people leave the organization
to build a business around ideas perceived during their employment
with Ericsson, e.g. Lumentis and Qyeton. This may have been one of

An increasing established working on give employees to develop necessarily fit

number of companies are programs to the opportunity ideas that don't in with the core business the reasons for Ericsson to start Ericsson Business Innovation, a separate legal entity giving Ericsson employees the opportunity to start a venture based on their idea in exchange for an equity stake in the venture. Having spun off several companies such as ConnectThings (acquired by Airclic Inc. in February 2001), Ericsson Business Innovation seems successful.

An increasing number of established companies are working on programs to give employees the opportunity to develop ideas that don't necessarily fit in with the core business or which might be a threat to existing business but have the potential to create value for the company. They are doing this both to keep in touch with new webs of innovation for strategic renewal and to retain talented employees.

In the past, internal ventures were often not part of or the result of a structured and formalized internal venturing strategy which delayed their progress significantly as they had to deal with the resistance to change of organizational bureaucracies that were built for serving mature markets and not for immature ones. This is changing however, with an increasing number of established companies offering structured internal venturing programs. There are no best practices yet but many established companies are experimenting to find the best way. Time will tell whether offering formal internal venturing programs increases the success rate of these internal ventures.

Internal venturing is an old concept that has been reinvented with the arrival of the internet. After the internet revolution, established companies have woken up. They messed up with the internet revolution but don't want to miss out on the internet evolution. Especially for companies that have seen their industry turned around with the arrival of the internet, internal venturing is a way to plug themselves into new webs of innovation arising in their industry and make sure their company makes it to become a dot corp.

Having the internet activities in a separate internal venture, an e-venture, brings several advantages. Most important is that as the internet is a disruptive technology and the market is immature, e-ventures need freedom and flexibility to hook up with the relevant webs of innovation. Later these companies could either be spun off (sold or taken public) or spun in back to lines of business. Another advantage is that with one, or several, clearly structured e-ventures the company remains an overview of its e-strategy whereas before, companies used to have several parts of their organization working on their own e-strategy. Delta Airlines for instance had functional areas that had their own online strategies and initiatives with little co-ordination, little accountability, and sub-optimization of assets. The company has since set up a separate e-venture, allowing ownership, focus, and fast development.[1] This has increased the chances for the company not to miss out on the internet evolution.

This chapter will explore one of the three key networked innovation components – internal venturing. It discusses the history of internal venturing, what type of people use it and how it works in practice. A case study on Lucent Technologies shows how the company has structured its internal venturing program.

The return of intrapreneurship

Within most companies bureaucracy offers the opportunity for so-called "skunk works" (working on something new without informing the management). But a lot of these skunk works were shot down just as they reached an interesting point in their development. The result is that the skunk-workers spend a lot of time defending themselves against bureaucracy instead of plugging themselves into webs of innovation.

There are also many examples of skunk-workers who left their company to start their own company to continue their former skunk work. Think of the Xerox examples in Chapter 1. Besides that there are also a huge number of skunk-workers who gave up, as they didn't want to risk everything on setting up a start-up. That's actually a large number of people. You won't find die-hard entrepreneurs within established companies. They would never take working at an established giant into consideration. But a start-up within an established company might be an attractive option for skunk-workers. You will be amazed by how many of these people there are. They might even outnumber the entrepreneurs.

The whole concept of internal venturing is not entirely new. In the eighties, Gifford Pinchot coined the term "intrapreneurship" for entrepreneurs within large organizations.[2] The concept was great but there aren't too many successful examples of companies that have successfully implemented his ideas.

Perhaps Pinchot did not choose the right time to introduce his ideas. In the eighties, when his book was published, established companies didn't see a clear threat on their horizon and had no particular reason to work on internal venturing. However, this changed with the arrival of the internet in the early nineties. In the years after its arrival established companies became aware of the threats and opportunities offered by the internet. Meanwhile new value was created by new companies, often started by former employees of established companies. Talented employees left the established companies and created value in which the established companies had no stake. So the threat and opportunities offered by the internet, potential gains, and employee retention seemed to be the main reasons driving the increase in internal venturing programs.

An increasing number of established companies have been starting internal venturing programs with titles such as "incubator," "new business group" or "launchpad," reviving Mr Pinchot's concept. The internet revolution brought us many new companies such as eBay, Yahoo, and Amazon. In the second act, the internet evolution, the established companies get a second chance to create value out of the internet. Other players might arise in the next wave that will make the internet change our daily lives. With this next wave it might be the established companies that are striking back as the internet becomes business as usual.

Initiatives to support and stimulate internal venturing, starting companies within existing companies, have been around in established companies but were usually fragmented over business units and never stayed around for long. Ericsson, for instance had several initiatives spread over several business units before it started Ericsson Business Innovation. These initiatives were often initiated on a business unit level but not as part of an overall structured effort on participating in webs of innovation. Ericsson's Business Innovation houses about 20 companies both from within and outside of Ericsson (January 2001).[3]

The majority of internal venturing programs have only been around for a few years so it is too early to be able to state whether they have been successful or not. What one can state though is that the number of initiatives is clearly increasing, mostly due to the arrival of the internet. As opposed to earlier efforts in the past this time the efforts seem to be a structured part of an overall effort to become part of webs of innovation that way ensuring the sustainability of the programs.

By setting up these programs a start-up atmosphere is created within the company's boundaries, allowing the ventures to become part of the relevant webs of innovation without being disturbed by internal bureaucracy or politics. This gives the ventures "breathing space" to work on what I like to call "business innovation." By this, I mean turning the role of the company within the web of innovation into a profitable and sustainable business, creating a business model out of a concept, defining customers, partners, revenue streams, etc. It might turn out that this business model in some way competes with the existing business. Being under the "wings" of an internal venturing program it can be ensured that this is a market driven process, not an internal driven one. "Breathing space" is needed.

Barnes and Noble versus Amazon

A good example is described by Harvard Business School Professor Rosabeth Moss Kanter in her book *e-Volve* with the barnesandnoble.com case.[4] In 1995 Amazon.com launched its online bookstore. Initially, the industry did not consider it a serious threat. Neither did bookstore chain Barnes and Noble. How could a small start-up have any serious impact on Barnes and Noble's dominance?

However in 1996, Barnes and Noble's CEO Stephen Riggio decided to start an online store as well. More as a nice-to-have than must-have it seemed, as minimal resources were allocated to its development. The website went live in 1997. Its design reflected the ideas behind its existing business. The Barnes and Noble stores stimulates people to spend a lot of time, there are often couches where customers can sit down and read, authors give speeches and in the bigger stores there often is a coffee shop. The website had message boards, online author chats, and other places encouraging visitors to spend time. This was completely different from the Amazon site. Amazon became popular because it enabled customers to do things they couldn't do before. It meant lower prices, more stock (no two to three weeks' wait when books had to be ordered), and the convenience of home delivery. All of this made Barnes and Noble aware that Amazon was a serious threat to its business by offering things that the customer couldn't get in its store. Developing this new business within the existing business would not work as this seemed to be another business model. Breathing space was needed. Therefore, the two parts were separated in two stages.

The first stage, in 1997, was having its own separate geographic location and leadership. Still the existing business interfered a lot with the unit. The next stage was in 1998 when a joint venture with Bertelsmann invested several hundreds of dollars, resulting in the company being set up as a separate legal entity. Barnesandnoble.com had its own CEO, the partners kept a 41 percent stake and in 1999 the company floated. Over time it grew into one of the larger players in the field.

Benefits of a formal internal venturing program

Barnesandnoble.com is a good example of the need for breathing space. However, "breathing space" is not all that is needed; a place where there is expertise with business innovation is also required. With innovation in mature markets business innovation is often not needed as the business model is already known. Especially for technology companies business innovation is key though as often ideas are conceived by technical employees. These employees love working on new technologies to find out the new new thing but when it comes to perfecting these and building a business out of it they usually lack the required skills. Offering a formal internal venturing program offers a place to go for these people and makes sure the company doesn't miss out on potential new revenue streams.

Often these programs allow and even stimulate external financing as it is a good way to validate the company. Now the dot coms have shown the investor world that it's hard to build up a brand, customer base,

A structured
it less people
(people leaving
changing
the company)
with larger

approach makes
dependent
the company or
positions within
and therefore
chances of
sustainability

distribution channel, and credibility, the internal ventures are attractive to invest in for investors as the established companies can offer all of these tangible and intangible assets. By having the e-business in separate internal ventures the management can operate autonomously while leveraging the benefits the "parent company" offers, such as infrastructure, financial resources, brand, distribution channel, customer base, and industry expertise. From an established company perspective, external financing of the ventures also reduces the risk, when an investment is lost it is not all at the cost of the company. With the same amount of money it enables the established company to bet on more horses. For outside investors the fact that an internal venture is a separate entity gives the opportunity more easily to value the internal venture. The downside of having external investors invest in these ventures is that when a company decides to spin-in the venture, the external investors might be an obstacle as these investors can have other plans with the venture.

The final advantage that I want to discuss is a potential one. A structured approach makes it less people dependent (people leaving the company or changing positions within the company) and therefore with larger chances of sustainability. Although there is not too much experience with structured internal venturing programs it might be that these schemes become an internal "Silicon Valley" as they will create informal networks of people. However, as most structured approaches started recently, as you can see in Table 3.1, that is in the future. Working out the best way to do internal venturing and achieving successes is the first challenge.

Take for instance British Telecom (BT). In April 2000 it started with an internal venturing program called Brightstar that was launched in December 2000. In March 2001 Brightstar had 12 ventures in its program that were "in incubation" and 4 that had been launched. Until

TABLE 3.1 Structured internal venturing programs

Established company	Internal venturing program	Since
Adobe	The Idea Studio	1999
British Telecom	Brightstar	2000
Ericsson	Ericsson Business Innovation	2000
Lucent	Lucent New Ventures Group	1997
United Parcel Service	e-Ventures	2000

the ventures get funding employees remain on BT's payroll. The funding usually comes from BT (£200,000–£800,000) and a venture capitalist.[5] It also takes companies into incubation that originate from outside BT. BT is planning on opening offices in Malaysia and exploring opportunities to set up offices in Boston as well for Brightstar. As of March 2001 25 people were employed at Brightstar.

Brightstar is located in the UK in Adastral Park, BT's technology park. Many inventions have been made in the park but often not applied in any business way or the inventors left the park to start their own business built on the ideas they came up with while working at BT. That way BT lost talented employees and missed out on value creation. That was one of the key reasons for the company to start its Brightstar incubator. The other one is to make sure BT remains part of relevant webs of innovation. Support for Brightstar by BT CEO Sir Peter Bonfield ensured that Brightstar was created.

BT's Brightstar is just one of the many examples of an established company that have set up an internal venturing program. After missing out on the internet revolution established companies are trying not to miss out on the internet evolution on value created by good ideas within the organization and to retain employees. One way to enter webs of innovation is through internal venturing. That explains the return of intrapreneurship. As mentioned earlier, an increasing number of companies are starting structured internal venturing programs. It is an old concept that so far has been more successful as a concept than in practice. Now, thanks to the arrival of the internet, established companies are trying to turn this concept into reality. Just as all companies take time to grow and mature, so do these programs and the companies are finding out that it is not easy.

The difficulties faced

There are many companies talking about starting internal venturing but not actually doing it. Internal venturing is not easy and takes time to develop, as I learned through talking to executives responsible for these programs. Much time is spend in buy-in within the firm, getting the funds and setting up the operations. Millions of dollars have been spent on strategic consultants such as the Boston Consulting Group or McKinsey to work on the concept and structures only. Unfortunately it is after the launch that it really starts. Selecting ventures, growing them, assuring next rounds of financing, spinning them in or off and so on. These are often things for which many established companies have little in-house expertise and this is also true of the consultants. The majority of these internal venturing programs have not been around that long and therefore it is hard to measure their success. Ultimately, the aim is to create successful internal ventures that create value for the company. Time will tell how successful these internal venturing programs have been.

When these initiatives are started they draw a lot of attention within the company. A combination of a sexy name, internet, coverage in internal publications and intrapreneurship assures this. But keeping up continuous top management attention for instance is hard but essential to keep these programs going. If there is no linkage between the internal venturing program and the annual objectives of the executives (e.g. aiming for at least spinning in two ideas a year that were a result of internal venturing) these programs will slowly die.

The road to success of the ventures can be long. A strong internal venturing program manager can be essential to ensure that support at top management level is sustained. Most internal venturing program managers are recruited from within the companies' senior management. At Lucent, for instance Tom Uhlman, former Senior VP corporate development, heads the Lucent New Ventures Group.

However, recruiting from within the company's senior management for the internal venturing program manager can also lead to problems. Quite often these senior managers have been within the established company for a while. They achieved their senior positions as they were good at managing mature businesses. However, being good at managing mature businesses does not necessarily mean being good in immature businesses as those two types of businesses require different skills. One solution is to look for a senior manager who also has experience as an entrepreneur, VC, or in the relevant field. Tom Uhlman for instance worked in Silicon Valley for Hewlett Packard.

An often quoted problem is that the established company thinking is that if you seriously want to build a new business fast you shouldn't skimp on funding and other resources.[6] This is certainly true for established businesses. However this can be fatal for new businesses. First, it takes a while to get to a positive cash flow, even if you invest a lot of money. Second, a tight budget leads to discipline; too much money can be disastrous as many start-ups showed after the hype. In an interview a former employee of former online clothing store Boo.com stated "It is not often you get to spend $130 million. It was the best fun… The atmosphere in the business was great. We thought we were the next Microsoft, so profits didn't matter."[7] Completely focusing on being a first mover the company launched in 18 countries simultaneously. Its executives often held team meetings in expensive restaurants and flew first class. The industry joke became that the company was managed according to the three C's; Champagne, Caviar, and Concorde. Too much money is not necessarily a good thing.

Instead of one-off payments, many internal venturing programs have copied the venture capital financing model of small milestone-related investments instead of a few large investments at once. This means not thinking budget but thinking milestone-oriented decision making – milestones being achievements such as first customer, first version, or partnerships. When a milestone is not achieved the investment is not made. This way a certain discipline is put upon the venture and it is also the best way to monitor the company. Knowing that only a small number of ventures eventually become successful the company can bet on several horses by making relatively small investments and at a lower risk. This method of working is completely opposite to the traditional established companies approach of deciding upon a project, allocating a budget, and pushing it through at all costs (see Figure 3.1).

An example of a company that found that changed from the traditional method towards the venture capital milestone approach is Adobe. Prior

Instead of **one-off payments**, many internal venturing programs have copied the venture capital financing model of **small milestone-related investments instead** of a few **large investments** at once.

to starting its internal venturing program "the Idea Studio," Adobe had another internal venturing program called "The Greenhouse" that failed. The failure was due to pushing through ideas without clearly defined stages or milestones. The company learned from this and ideas must now have a business model and set forth measurable stages before they go into incubation. Its advisory board monitors each step and goals must be reached before proceeding to the next stage.[8]

Instead of flooding the venture with money the company might as well put more of an emphasis on providing them with non-financial things such as access to its customer base, leveraging the brand, its distribution channel, or expertise. Things such as access to research facilities are of very high value to a start-up. It is also important to ensure that there are enough incentives in place (both financial and non-financial) for the participants in the venture, such as options on shares in the venture. That is of much more value for the venture in order to become part of a web of innovation than a slick office, house

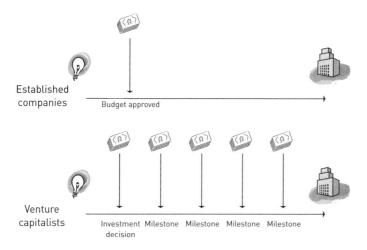

FIGURE 3.1 Traditional budget financing of established companies versus the venture capital milestone approach

style, and a lot of 9–5 employees. Having too many employees will often slow down operations. With a dedicated but smaller number of employees, almost understaffing, stimulates a focus and efficiency. When progress is made, new hires can be recruited. Keeping tight control of resources leads to discipline.

Besides overthrowing an internal venture with money another often-made mistake seems to be that the development of the venture focuses entirely on using internal resources. This places emphasis on the relation between the company and the venture instead of on continuously thinking of how the venture performs within the web. Especially when the venture is dominated by technical people, the focus tends to be technology led instead of market led. It is preferable, therefore, to use experienced commercial managers instead of technical people with limited management experience. The ultimate test to see how a venture is validated within a web of innovation is interacting with players in the web of innovation. Therefore a venture needs to start making new customers, forming partnerships, and so on as early as it can. In addition, less formal ways of plugging into webs of innovation should not be overlooked, such as attending networking events, conferences and using tools made available by the internet, such as mailing lists and newsgroups.

At **www.alphaworks.ibm.com** IBM has created a community hosting several of its early stage technologies that visitors to the website can download, experiment with, and give feedback on. The visitors, often "early adaptors," think it is cool to see new stuff in an early stage and IBM enjoys the benefits of free input. Since its launch in August 1996 it has become very popular; in October 1998 over 1 million downloads were logged. It has helped to commercialize several products such as WebSphere Application Server, VisualAge for Java (the HPJC integration), Lotus BeanMachine, Bamba, Aglets Workbench, Hot

Video, Interactive Network Dispatcher, NetRexx, PanaramaIX, and Webrunner Toolkit, among others. Current releases include a wide range of Java-based technologies, XML tools and open source code. The website community has paid off for IBM. Plugging into webs of innovation at an early stage is very important.

Another challenge seems to be decision making. The vice president of a large public European high tech company, responsible for internal venturing told me that the biggest problem at his company was getting the OK for new businesses. It is difficult to select and choose internal ventures. Many companies therefore choose to work with investment boards, forming committees with the relevant executives needed to make the decision. Choosing the right people to sit on these committees is tough. A combination is sought of people who have credibility within the organization, have expertise in the business the venture is in and understand how immature markets work. The right investment board members are scarce. People with credibility within the organization often have experience that is based on the existing business; few of them have experience with new immature markets. Often they have their own agenda of focal areas. Nevertheless one of this type is needed. Other types could be veteran intrapreneurs or highly respected senior researchers. Some companies invite third parties such as venture capitalists, academics, or consultants. Texas Instruments for instance works closely with venture capital partner Hambrecht and Quist for representatives on its investment board.[9]

The majority of these internal venturing programs that are nurturing these programs are start-ups themselves. They still have to refine and work out the best way to do things. Not all established companies have the patience to do this and therefore some established companies hook up with companies that focus on helping established companies with their e-ventures – know as e-builders.

The rise of e-builders

The use of "e-builders" began with established companies teaming up with venture capitalists on their e-ventures. Many of the well-known venture capitalists in Silicon Valley were visited by executives of established companies in around 1998–1999 seeking help, which resulted in these venture capitalists helping set up their e-ventures. Table 3.2 provides some examples.

TABLE 3.2 E-ventures set up with the involvement of venture capitalists

Established company	Venture capital company	E-venture
Kmart	Softbank Venture Capital	Bluelight.com
Nordstrom	Benchmark Capital	Nordstrom.com
Procter & Gamble	Institutional Venture Partners	Reflect.com
Wal-Mart	Accel Partners	Wal-Mart.com

At the same time, consultants and investment banks were increasingly being asked by customers to help them on their e-ventures. This lead to the rise of e-builders that combine consulting and financial knowledge. These companies either help in setting up e-ventures for single companies or combine several established companies into one new e-venture.

The well-known Silicon Valley venture capital company Kleiner Perkins Caufield & Byers (with an impressive portfolio consisting of among others Compaq, Intuit, Netscape, Lotus, Sun Microsystems, Amazon.com, and Symantec) for instance started an e-builder, eVolution Global Partners, that will help clients carve out internet-related business from their current ones. They partnered with strategic consulting firm Bain and buyout firm Texas Pacific Group. A similar example is a company called Accel-KRR Internet started by another

Silicon Valley based venture capital firm called Accel.Partners and Kohlberg Kravis Roberts & Co (KRR), a competitor of the Texas Pacific Group. In Europe Accel-KRR joined forces with Europ@Web in e-builder AKA Technology. Another e-builder is the $300 million backed iFormation Group, consisting of venture capital company General Atlantic Partners, consulting firm The Boston Consulting Group and investment bank Goldman Sachs. In Europe, Antfactory is doing the same thing in alliance with consulting firm Accenture. As shown, they are all well-backed, well-known companies.

An example of an e-venture created by an e-builder is MarketMile. eVolution invested $16 million in this US marketplace for business products and services aimed at mid-sized companies in November 2000. This e-venture was founded in August of that same year by American Express and Ventro (which builds e-marketplaces).[10] Other examples are eMac Digital, set up by Accel-KRR and fast food chain McDonalds or GroceryWorks.com, by supermarket Safeway and Accel-KRR.[11]

These collaborations are very interesting but like the e-ventures they are building, they are still start-ups themselves, so they are still in the process of finding out the best way to do things. Critics mention the lack of operational expertise and dominance of consultants. Another aspect they mention is that established companies are afraid of sharing equity in their e-venture from the start. In practice it might be that the e-builder gets such a large share that investing in next rounds of financing is not attractive to outside investors. These e-builders are often alliances itself which can sometimes lead to politics among the alliance members. So far, few deals have seen the light. Believers in the model say that this can be explained because it takes time to get these deals done. Time will tell whether these e-builders will be successful.

Internal venturing is new to many companies and not all of them want to do it themselves, so they join up with e-builders to set up their e-ventures. Whether built in-house or by e-builders, once e-ventures are built the next issue is how to take things further – spinning in or spinning out.

Spinning in or out

Established companies have often considered the concept of internal venturing programs and getting internal buy-in in some depth. After launching these programs, they discover that internal venturing is difficult. As they learn how to select and invest in internal ventures and grow them at some point some internal ventures make it to the stage that they're ready to exit the internal venturing program and to enter adulthood. As the majority of internal venturing programs have not been around long, patterns with these exits are not too clear.

However, two main approaches can be observed; spinning in and spinning out. If spinning in is the case, the e-venture is integrated with the existing organization after development. This is often the case when it adds value to an existing business unit or when it is complementary to existing business units. The e-venture is then either integrated into an existing line of business or a new business line is created. In case of spin-outs e-ventures are spun out of the organization and the company cashes in via share sales or trade sale. This is usually done when an e-venture falls outside the company's strategic focus.

An example of spin-in is Citigroup Inc., which decided to collapse Citi f/I (its pure play bank) and Direct Access (its online banking program), into a single service that will deliver service through a mix of electronic and physical channels.[12] Well-known examples of spin-outs include the flotation of internet service provider Freeserve by Dixons in the UK at £1.5 billion, online financial news provider MarketWatch.com by CBS and online news provider ZDNet by Ziff-Davis.

During a workshop on internal venturing with several well-known companies participating I found that spinning in a venture is hard. Its success very much depends on the degree to which the existing business is engaged in the internal venturing program. It seems important to have the existing business engaged in an early stage as the company might in a later stage acquire the internal venture and some of its assets can be essential to the internal venture. One way of doing this is for the existing business to participate in the due diligence phase. Later on people from the existing business sit on the venture's board or become a sponsor for it. One of the reasons that having somebody with prior senior management experience from within the company is that this person usually has credibility and a network within the existing business. That way internal venturing management can proactively work on marketing of the ventures to the existing business, creating awareness and interest. When it is time for the ventures to exit, the existing businesses are aware of their existence and might decide to have the internal venture spun-in.

TABLE 3.3 Spin-out or spin-in?

	Outside of strategic focus	Within strategic focus
New business	Spin-off	Spin-in: new business unit created
Complementing existing business		Spin-in: integrated into existing business unit

Established often considered internal programs and buy-in in some launching these discover that

companies have the concept of venturing **getting internal depth.** After programs, **they** internal venturing **is difficult.**

Whether spinning out or in is the best solution varies according to each situation. A good example is that of stockbroker Charles Schwab. In 1995 the company launched a separate venture, e.Schwab, which offered online trading at a very low price and with very basic support. The venture became a great success. However, over time, Schwab's customers also wanted to be able to use the internet for their transactions, and the e.Schwab customers wanted the Schwab benefits of branches and telephone support. The company decided to combine the two into e.Schwab. Nowadays the company has a larger share of online share trading than competitor E*Trade.

Over time successes with internal venturing will become apparent, as will failures. There will probably be more failures than successes as a venture is more likely to fail than to succeed. The causes of failure differ. It could be a result of key people leaving, the venture not making it to the next round, or the market responding differently than was expected. It is often a combination of these factors. Take for instance WorldofFruit.com, a web-based exchange for fresh products. Launched in November 1999 by Fyffes, Europe's second biggest banana importer, the company announced in January 2001 that it would freeze its investment in the e-venture as the company was having difficulties raising money as it failed to attract external users outside of the Fyffes group.[13] Although the focus always seems to be on successes, failures are normal in immature markets. In Silicon Valley people state that only 1 out of 20 companies succeeds. However, many established companies have a hard time acknowledging that. Established companies tend not to give up easily. Even when things have failed they go on keeping up appearances. However, Fyffes clearly showed itself to be different by freezing its investment.

With the arrival of the internet, intrapreneurship made its return. Although it's a great concept, in practice internal venturing is hard.

Remember, like the ventures they are nurturing, these programs are start-ups themselves and are still finding the best model. As the number of "exits" of start-ups increases, it will also become more clear which paths are preferred. However these things develop, the core asset in these ventures remains the same – good staff.

Entrepreneurs are different people than managers. However, a very small percentage of employees knows how to combine entrepreneurial characteristics with established company skills; the intrapreneur. To better understand this type let's compare the intrapreneur with the entrepreneur.

Intrapreneurs versus entrepreneurs

Established companies tend to opt for an idea-driven approach in contrast with immature market companies, which are more people driven. Within established companies the right planning, detailed budgets, and daily reports are there to guarantee minimal risk. That's great for existing stuff but for new stuff you minimalize risk by working with the right people, not by working with GANTT charts. At the end of the day it's about execution and execution is people. Creating new stuff is done by *entrepreneurial* people.

It is difficult to find true entrepreneurs within established companies. Usually these people are characterized as persistent, stubborn, passionate, energetic, and hard working. Is there a place for someone like that within an established company where the focus is on doing things "the company way" as opposed to the true entrepreneur who wants to change "the company way"?

That's where the intrapreneur comes in. As Gifford Pinchot, who coined the term in his book *Intrapreneuring* this person has all the characteristics of a true entrepreneur but also that of an enthusiastic and smart networker; tactic, nice, humble, helpful, eager to learn, communicative.[14] Usually they have a track record of building new things in the company, like a new brand or a new office. As a professional they have to be multitaskers, combining both technical and commercial skills. This type of person is rare and essential for companies in order to survive.

Take for instance an intrapreneur such as Art Fry, who invented the Post-It Note. It's probably hard to imagine a time without Post-It Notes but there was! It all started when Fry discovered an adhesive that was invented at 3M but not being used. The adhesive, combined with small pieces of paper turned out to be very useful as a bookmark to put in his hymnal without damaging the paper. After he used it in the office once in a report for a colleague he got an enthusiastic reply. That drove him to take it further. But then he hit his head against the established company thinking; it was perceived that his idea would cause huge waste and that coating paper with the special adhesive would prove difficult. Mr Fry proved to be a true intrapreneur by not giving up, instead he came up with the creative idea of giving away free samples and people soon got addicted to the Post-It Notes. He then suddenly took back all the samples. Soon after doing so he found that the samples had done their work; everybody was convinced of the potential. Nowadays several million of the pads are sold each year.[15] Without an intrapreneur as Mr Fry behind it the product would never have become so successful.

Although intrapreneurs are passionate about the company that employs them they also see a lot of opportunities that are not being explored or exploited by the company.

Although intrapreneurs are passionate about the company that employs them they also see a lot of opportunities that are not being explored or exploited by the company. However, this envisioning of opportunities does not make them want to leave the company. On the contrary, they are passionate to take on these opportunities for the sake of their company just as Mr Fry did. Bureaucracy, internal politics and initial rejection will not stop these intrapreneurs from preaching their ideas throughout the organization and most importantly, getting things done.

Having one person championing an idea is key as the example of Art Fry showed. But what also helps is having an executive manager who supports the intrapreneur. One intrapreneur told me that this was one of the secrets behind his effort. The supporting executive believed in his ideas and provided him with a team and all the other resources he needed. Intrapreneurs need to be taken under an executive's wing to be able to do their thing.

An increasing number of executives are starting to see the importance of intrapreneurs for strategic renewal of the firm. Usually, one intrapreneur was behind an idea that was initially perceived as a weird idea but later turned out to form a huge part of the revenues. Take for instance Sony's PlayStation. As early as the eighties Ken Kutaragi had a vision about a game machine. However, the management team at Sony did not see games as a serious consumer product. But Kutaragi did not give up. Finally he won the support of the then CEO Norio Ohga and the PlayStation was born. After its launch in 1994 it became one of the company's top selling products. In 1998 the PlayStation was providing 40 percent of Sony's operating profits.[16] Without Kutaragi's persistence, these profits would not have been achieved.

There are several cases of companies where a significant part of the revenues are derived from a product that was championed by an intrapreneur. Take Intel and the microprocessor. It used to be a semiconductor memory company and also made application-specific chips that performed logical operations in its customers' products. At the time, this was a great business but these specially designed chips had one drawback; when changes in a feature set of products had to be made, the entire chip had to be redesigned. Intel engineer Ted Hoff met with a young engineer, Masatoshi Shima, who had thought of a chip that would process multipurpose commands. So, in order to change the features of a product like a calculator, you would just make minor changes in read-only memory. Ted Hoff hired the engineer and the necessary other team members and under his guidance they created the first microprocessor, Intel's 4004.[17] The majority of Intel's revenue now comes from microprocessor sales.

Formalizing internal venturing programs is a way to help these intrapreneurs to draw attention to their ideas more quickly. Although it was invented in 1994, the first Bluetooth (a device that replaces cables with radio wave based communication between electronic devices) will hit the shelves in 2001 as it took Jaap Haartsen, Bluetooth's inventor, several years to convince everybody within the company of its potential. That drastically slowed down its development. This kind of delay can be fatal to companies. Speed is increasingly important. As Cisco CEO John Chambers is often quoted: "It's not about small companies versus big companies but about fast versus slow companies." Formalized internal venturing programs can help to speed up things by offering one place to go with ideas and within that place providing the appropriate environment.

To give you an example of how things can be delayed by not having the appropriate environment, Jeff Dodge and Gord Larose of Channelware, a Nortel venture that was spun off in the summer of 2000, told in *Fastcompany* magazine about their confrontations with the bureaucracy within Nortel when working on their venture and wanting to hire people.[18] Larose was told that he could not use Nortel's jobs database to hire staff for Channelware because he was not a hiring manager, since nobody reported to him. But he couldn't hire people to report to him unless he was allowed to use the database to hire them. The situation became worse when Nortel declared a freeze on recruitment. But that didn't stop these intrapreneurs from coming up with a creative solution. Dodge formed Channelware, incorporated it under his own name, hired people and claimed their salaries at Nortel as a consulting expense. However, it greatly delayed their operations. This could have been avoided if there had been a place for them to go which provided the appropriate environment.

Speeding things up is not the only issue. Retaining talented employees is also very important, and empowering them in their intrapreneurial needs. If you don't empower the intrapreneur, they are likely to leave your organization to start their own company – which one day might become the new Cisco or Intel. It might even become the leader in your industry and make your company obsolete, or it could mean that your company misses out on value creation.

Often these intrapreneurs do not become "true" entrepreneurs as they do not want to risk everything. They prefer the stability and reliability of the established company behind them. Often, while in the venture, their salary continues to be paid. Nortel employees who are part of internal ventures earn their regular salary, plus a milestone-dependent bonus every six months. When a company is spun off its team receives 15–30 percent of the shares in the company.[19] Although this stake for the team is not what it would have been if they had operated as "true entrepreneurs" it can still be very attractive, while they take less risk and keep benefits such as salary and so on. As Mark Goldstein, Former CEO of Bluelight.com (the e-venture of Kmart), stated in an interview: "At Bluelight.com, we have a floor: we are Kmart's e-commerce company, so our worst-case scenario is to become a part of Kmart again."[20]

Another advantage is that internal venturing programs within established companies tend to be more patient than external venture capitalists; they are less short time driven. Especially within a non-stable financial market this offers the best combination of entrepreneurship and corporate risk aversion.[21]

The authors of the book *Radical innovation: how mature companies can outsmart upstarts* studied several cases of internal ventures and found that it is difficult to define success factors. One thing was clear though; a formalized internal venturing program can provide the intrapreneurs with what they need; an environment where they have freedom to do what they are best at.

Intrapreneurs are special people. There aren't many of them in companies, although possibly more than you think. They might even outnumber entrepreneurs. To thrive best these people need somewhere in the organization they can go to with their ideas. Established companies are still working out the best way to facilitate internal venturing. Success or failure of the internal venture depends on the quality of the intrapreneurs behind it. One company that has been relatively active for a while in internal venturing is the Lucent New Ventures Group.

Lucent New Ventures Group

In 1997 Lucent started its New Ventures Group. The idea was championed by the president of Bell Labs, Dan Stanzione. He saw the importance of having a vehicle to deal with internal ventures in 1995. He delegated this idea to Tom Uhlman, then senior vice president of corporate development, who formed a team. Together they also supported the first venture, Elemedia, which was internally acquired in July 1999 by Lucent's Switching and Access

Solutions Group. By October 1997, the Lucent Executive Council approved the step of making the New Ventures Group (NVG) Business Unit. This group then had an equal status with the other ten Lucent divisions. By March 2001, NVG had created 33 ventures. Forty venture capital companies and 20 strategic corporate investors had invested about $300 million in this portfolio of ventures. NVG had an internal rate of return of about 65 percent over the three years to the beginning of 2001.

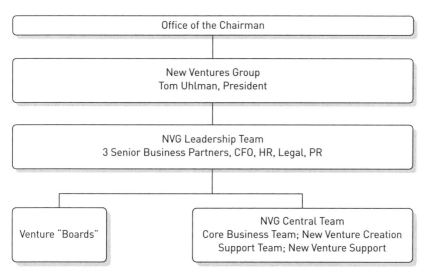

FIGURE 3.2   Lucent New Ventures Group organizational structure

The idea was to have this group as an innovation model to:

● add value/growth

● extract value from technology

● change culture.

Ultimately,
of creating
the company
employees,
the concept

it is a matter

value for

and retaining

and of taking

to reality.

In March 2001, three internal ventures had been spun into Lucent, three had been closed and 26 were still active. Lucent continues to pay salaries of employees who join a venture but instead of the yearly performance bonus these employees get stock equity in the venture. This forms an incentive but also a way to retain the employees for a longer time via vesting. Vesting is an agreed period with an employer indicating how long it takes before his or her options or shares in a company become his or hers. This is to ensure an employee's commitment.

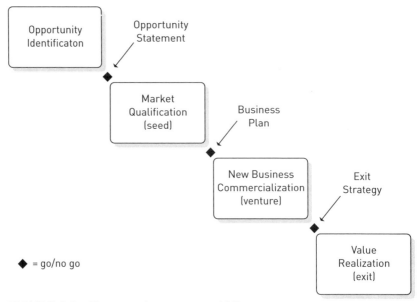

FIGURE 3.3   The venturing process at NVG

The future

After initial caution, it now seems that many companies are keen to explore internal venturing. Some of them are even starting to "walk the talk" as they are announcing internal venturing programs. Great concepts are presented, beautiful buildings are assigned and strategic consultants are making a lot of money. However, ultimately, it is a matter of creating value for the company and retaining employees, and of taking the concept to reality. Many internal venturing programs are in a very early stage. They have the concept but are still working out how to turn it into reality. Time will tell whether established companies will succeed in nurturing internal ventures with disruptive ideas.

Conclusion

Internal venturing is one of the key components of networked innovation. With the arrival of the internet, an increasing number of established companies are starting internal venturing programs to nurture start-ups within an established company environment, thus providing a place to go for intrapreneurs within the organization. For the established company the aim is to ensure it captures the value created by good ideas in the organization, retain employees and not miss out in the internet evolution.

It is not easy to set up internal venturing programs and as established companies have only recently begun to embark on such programs, they are still learning about them. Many internal venturing programs have copied the venture capital funding model, in which receiving small amounts of funding is related to achieving previously agreed milestones.

Some of the established companies do not have the patience to start these programs and work with external companies to build their e-ventures. When these internal ventures are fully developed, they can either be spun out or spun in. This depends on whether the internal venture is complementing existing business, creating new business within the strategic focus, or creating new business outside of the strategic focus.

However it is done, intrapreneurs are at the center of these internal ventures. When you look at key revenue streams of companies there is often an intrapreneur behind it who set the ball rolling. An increasing number of established companies is offering these intrapreneurs a place to go to.

In this chapter we looked at one of the networked innovation key components. Chapter 4 examines corporate venture capital – investing in start-ups by established companies.

Key points

 Think of major new products in your company. Was somebody championing it?

 Does your company have a structured internal venturing program? If so, why?

 How is your management team supporting intrapreneurship?

 What do ventures want and how does an established company add value to them?

 What are the barriers to a successful internal venturing program?

 Do you know of any intrapreneurs in your company?

 Would you or your employees have the opportunity to propose intrapreneurial plans?

 How does your company deal with making the internet part of the business?

 How can you ensure support from the core business?

Think of successful internal ventures in your company or other companies. How did they end up – spin-in or out?

 How are ideas that do not fit with your organization's current core business given consideration within your organization?

 Would you know of senior managers within your company that would support or champion intrapreneurship?

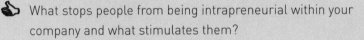 Does your company have the ability to take great ideas that are further developed into becoming a large new business?

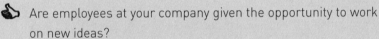 What stops people from being intrapreneurial within your company and what stimulates them?

 Are employees at your company given the opportunity to work on new ideas?

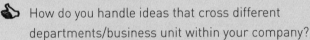 How are internal business ideas turned into reality in your company?

 How are intrapreneurial people incentivized within your organization?

 How do you handle ideas that cross different departments/business unit within your company?

How can you convince top management of the importance of internal venturing?

Does everyone in the organization see himself or herself involved in the innovation process?

Further information

At the website **www.websofinnovation.com** you can find additional resources on the subject, such as links to relevant articles, books, websites and over time this will be expanded. A mailing list on the subject of this chapter allows you to discuss it with other readers.

Notes

1. Hansell, Saul. "Now that we're still here, where do we go? Seven answers," *New York Times*, February 28, 2001.

2. Pinchot, Gifford. *Intrapreneuring*, Harper & Row, 1985.

3. D'Amico, Mary Lisbeth. "Spin-offs – the next wave," Tornado-Insider, edn. 21, Amsterdam, January 2001.

4. Moss Kanter, Rosabeth. *Evolve*, Harvard Business School Press, Boston, MA.

5. Harvey, Fiona. "How to make the most of a brilliant idea," *Financial Times*, December 6, 2000.

6. Clayton, James, Gambill, Bradley, and Harned, Douglas. "The curse of too much capital: building new businesses in large corporations," *McKinsey Quarterly*, Quarter 3, 1999.

7. "Wild Wild Web: searching for dotcom gold," *Financial Times*, October 9, 2000.

8. Eng, Sherri and Wray, Rick. "Cyberspace eggheads," *The Industry Standard Europe*, December 7, 2000.

9. Leifer, Richard *et al. Radical innovation; how mature companies can outsmart upstarts*, Harvard Business School Press, Cambridge, MA, 2000

10. Campbell, Katharine. "eVolution invests $16m in US Group," *Financial Times*, London, November 28, 2000.

11. Fleming, Charles. "Antfactory targets old economy turf," *The Wall Street Journal*, Dow Jones & Company Inc., August 22, 2000.

12. Koller, Lynn. Op. cit.

13. Barker, Thorold. "Fyffes freezes investment in internet venture," *Financial Times*, January 19, 2001.

14. Pinchot, Gifford. Op. cit.

15. Sims, Josh. "Stuck on you," *Financial Times*, December 2, 2000.

16. Takahashi, Dean. "Reinventing the intrapreneur," *Red Herring*, Red Herring Publications, San Francisco, September 2000.

17. "The revolutionary's handbook," The Strategos Institute, Menlo Park, CA, October 1999.

18. Lieber, Ron. "Start-ups – the 'inside' stories," Fast Company, Cambridge, March 2000.

19. Ibid.

20. "What will it take to win in the next phase of the new economy," Fastcompany.com, January 20, 2001.

21. Takahashi, Dean. "Reinventing the intrapreneur," *Red Herring*, Red Herring Publications, San Francisco, September 2000.

f o u r

[corporate venture capital]

IN JUNE 1999, APPLE INVESTED $12.5 MILLION IN JUNE IN
Akamai, a company set up by academics from Massachusetts Institute
of Technology. For their investment they received approximately 5
percent of the shares of the company. Akamai (pronounced AH kuh
my) is Hawaiian for intelligent, clever, and cool. With the flotation of
the company at the end of 1999 it turned out that their investment was
also pretty "akamai" as the share was worth about $1.3 billion after
flotation. A return on investment of 10,400 percent – not bad.

Apple is among the increasing number of established companies that
has set up venture capital activities. These activities are usually titled
"Corporate Venture Capital" (CVC). Although, just as Apple did with
its Akamai investment, profits are made, the big difference with
"normal" venture capital is that the objective is not only to create value
in the portfolio but also to create value in the parent company, a

The arrival of
driven the rise

venture capital

companies do

miss out

the internet has of corporate as established not want to on the internet evolution.

strategic objective. To stay in touch with the market and see new webs of innovation coming up that have a disruptive potential but also to plug the companies' products within these webs of innovation to ensure future revenue streams.

The arrival of the internet has driven the rise of corporate venture capital as established companies do not want to miss out on the internet evolution. In addition, CVC is increasing in popularity among start-ups. Now the hype is over, the start-ups are starting to appreciate the access to the tangible and intangible assets offered by established companies, especially distribution channel, expertise, and brand. These are all things that start-ups have found to take time to develop. CVC is one of the key components of networked innovation which we will explore in this chapter. We will look into the differences with "normal" venture capital, why it appeals to start-ups, in what flavours it comes and how the future for CVC looks like.

CVC is growing
The number of companies active in corporate venture capital is growing almost exponentially. In 1998 there were globally about 110 companies with venture capital arms or that make regular venture investments. In 2000 the number was 350, as shown in Figure 4.1. Although many established companies used to reject CVC as they either perceived it as a waste of management time or not their core business, these companies are increasingly changing their minds.

Established companies are starting to acknowledge the importance of being part of new webs of innovation for strategic renewal. They are finding out that CVC is not only about creating value within the portfolio but – more importantly – it is about creating value in the parent company. CVC is also about staying in touch with the market to see new

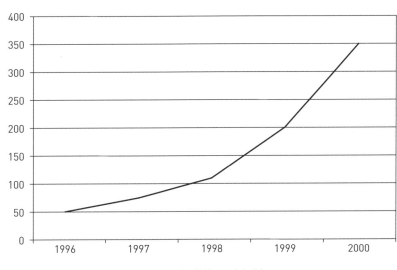

FIGURE 4.1 Corporations active in CVC worldwide

Source: **www.ft.com/ftsurveys/industry/sc23442.htm**

webs of innovation rise that might effect the core business because of its disruptive nature – catching the next wave via CVC. Another factor is stimulating the sales of its products by "plugging" the products into webs of innovation at an early stage, thus ensuring future growth.

That explains the growing involvement of CVC in venture capital deals. It's hard to measure CVC as these activities are not always very transparent. There are however companies specializing in gathering this type of information. VentureOne kindly showed me some of their data on the growing involvement of CVC in the US market. As you can see in Figure 4.2 there is a significant increase in the percentage of deals involving CVC, from 9 percent in 1994 to 27 percent in 2000.

Corporate venture capital has been around for a while. A working paper by Paul Gompers and Josh Lerner of the Harvard Business School provided me with some interesting historic background.[1] Whereas

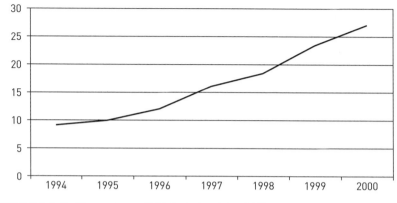

FIGURE 4.2 Percentage of VC deals involving CVC

Source: VentureOne

"normal" venture capital started in the mid-forties CVC started in the mid-sixties. The inspiration by corporates to start CVC funds came from VC-backed successes such as Digital Equipment, Memorex, Raychem, and others. During the late sixties and early seventies more than 25 percent of the Fortune 500 firms were giving CVC a try.

In 1973 though the market for IPOs (initial public offerings) was declining. That way the interest for "normal" VC funds started to decrease and CVC funds with that. The funds came back though in the late seventies and early eighties, then declined again after the 1987 stock market crash. From then until 1992 it continued to decline. After that the internet arrived, which attracted a lot of venture capital. In the mid-nineties many of these internet ventures began to go public, which woke up the established companies. Partly because of the attractive returns on investment but even more because of the big changes the internet was bringing. The changes seemed to have been initiated by these start-ups, which posed a threat to the established companies. Although they had missed the revolution, they did not want to miss the evolution, and found out that being part of webs of innovation was the best way to keep up and ensure future growth.

Although an increasing number of established players are working on CVC initiatives it is still a minority of all established companies, especially in Europe. The US seems to be ahead of Europe. Rough estimates state that CVC in the US is at least five times greater than CVC in Europe. However, an increasing number of established companies in Europe are starting CVC initiatives. Recent research found that a reason for not participating in a way of CVC by these companies was that they did not see the need to do so.[2] But slowly these companies are changing and acknowledging the need of CVC as a way to stay in touch with webs of innovation. Again, this is due to the internet revolution as established companies do not want to miss out on the internet evolution and ensure their future growth.

Some companies take it to the extreme in their desire to become part of webs of innovation. These companies find it so important to plug themselves in an early stage into these webs of innovation that they almost give products away. Take for instance business-incubator.com, an initiative by Sun, Cisco, and Oracle, the leading players in internet infrastructure and databases. They offer start-ups their products and services at a very low rate, without asking for shares or anything else. They do this to position themselves in the center of webs of innovation in as early a stage as possible in order to stay in touch with the market and see new webs of innovation come up, or even smarter, to create webs of innovation. They are making sure that the next wave of companies stimulate usage of their product and use it themselves. Companies do not usually change suppliers once they have matured – so they become attractive and loyal customers. By being in the webs of innovation in an early stage, these established companies ensure their future growth.

There are also cost advantages. By investing in new companies the company can bet on more horses for the same cost than if it carried out

When a

becomes really

can be acquired

becomes a way

potential

candidates at a

company

interesting **it**

and CVC

to incubate

acquisition

relatively

low cost.

the research and development itself. When a company becomes really interesting it can be acquired and CVC becomes a way to incubate potential acquisition candidates at a relatively low cost. Take for instance Ericsson and the company Swedish Radio Systems. Ericsson has held a stake in this company for sometime, which it has gradually increased. Until around 1984 Ericsson fully owned the company. Ericsson folded the company into its structure and it became the basis of the mobile systems business. In 1999, the mobile systems business was responsible for about 70 percent of the revenues.[3] Imagine the position if the company had not made these investments. This is a familiar pattern in the history of well-known companies. In Chapter 3 we saw that intrapreneurs were often at the basis of major current revenue streams but as the Ericsson example demonstrates, revenue can also come from companies an established company initially held a minority stake in. Chapter 5 examines acquisitions in greater detail and shows that established companies are increasingly using acquisitions as a cheap way to acquire competences.

Besides the strategic objectives that the majority of the established companies have, the potential for a high return on investment is also attractive although it is not usually the main objective. Since Reuters started its Greenhouse I fund in 1995 it has significantly contributed to the company's profits (see Figure 4.3). Two other funds have since been launched and their combined contribution to the group's profits grew from 2 percent in 1997 to 9 percent in 2000. The three funds have together invested about $432 million in about 83 companies (February 2001) in the finance, media, and network infrastructure, including well-known public companies such as Yahoo, Verisign, MarchFirst, Orchestream, and Phone.com. Besides these companies that went successfully public some of the companies in the portfolio were acquired such as Firefly by Microsoft and Infoseek by Disney.

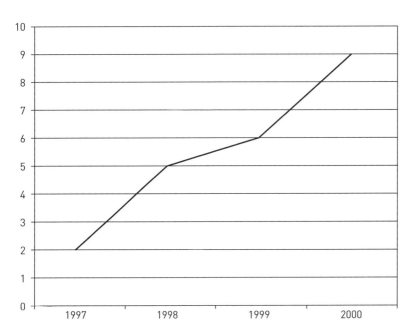

FIGURE 4.3 Percentage of Reuters group operating profits before tax

Source: Reuters Greenhouse Fund

Although these returns are attractive, that is not what has been the most important to Reuters. Its $1 million investment in Yahoo in 1995 paid off well as Yahoo floated in 1996 bringing it to a $848 million market capitalization in the first week. However, this was not Reuters' prime concern. Yahoo bought part of its content from Reuters. As Yahoo grew, this gave Reuters greater exposure and resulted in other portals also wanting Reuters to provide them with content. Nobody had heard of Reuters before in the US but that soon changed. Reuters ended up finding itself available on about 900 websites, viewed by an estimated 40 million users per month.[4] This has helped Reuters to become a dot corp, largely due to a $1 million investment.

The Reuters case clearly illustrates the difference with "normal" venture capital – creating value not only in the portfolio but also in the parent company.

The difference with "normal" venture capital

As opposed to "normal" venture capital, CVC is not, by definition, aimed only at generating profits; there is usually also a strategic element involved, often with several components. First, stimulating the usage of a company's product by plugging the product into new webs of innovation, so ensuring that the participants in the network use the product and/or stimulate sales of the product ensuring future growth. Second, to stay in touch with the market to see new webs of innovation rise that might affect the core business because of its disruptive nature. With all the changes that are likely in the internet evolution, CVC is a way to ensure that established companies become dot corps.

CVC is a great way to spot new webs of innovation and hooking up with start-ups at an early stage. Somehow established companies usually seem to hook up with other established companies and miss new webs of innovation. They seem to mingle more with established players in the existing business than with new players in new businesses. CVC is a good solution there. As Reuters former CEO Peter Job states: "The Greenhouse portfolio companies have provided Reuters with access to cutting edge technology without the risks and costs associated with in-house development."

The two aims, strategic versus ROI, are not mutually exclusive, although the balance differs. Roel Pieper, managing partner at Insight Ventures, told me that CVC tends to end up unbalanced in the middle on the spectrum between strategic and return on investment focus. According to him companies should focus on either one of the two.

Actually you can state that strategic and return on investment focus are not different at all. A focus on strategic means that it will generate more sales and profits for the parent company, rather than leading to a high valuation of the portfolio. So the question is more whether value creation should happen in the portfolio or whether the value creation should happen in the parent company.

Intel, for example, has a clear focus on value creation in the parent company – its venture capital activities have as their goal to stimulate businesses using Intel chips and understand emerging business models and technologies. In practice Intel makes a lot of money on its CVC activities as well. Intel realized a pretax profit of $3.7 billion in 2001 on the sale of some venture investments, it posted $10.5 billion in net income in 2000.[5] Although it has not always been their intent many companies are making a profit on their investments in the same way.

A study for the European Commission found that the motivation behind the majority of the CVC activities is value creation for the parent company. Table 4.1 shows three examples of motivations of CVC.[6] Nevertheless it is hard to fully separate these motivations as mutually independent. If successful, an investment will both earn a high IRR on the portfolio and create value for the parent company. If there is a low IRR on the portfolio the odds are that the technology will not be viable and the market entered will not be a growth area and therefore will not create value for the parent company. The majority of the companies therefore measure the successes of their CVC activities not only on strategic contribution but also on the IRR measure that "normal" VCs use as well. It is often about 25 percent on an annual basis. With the aim of value creation it is more a *continuum* than a case of "either/or." One does not exclude the other. However, being able to place your company's CVC activities on the continuum and having clarity on that is essential.

TABLE 4.1 Why CVC?

Company	Why it uses CVC	Fund name
Deutsche Bank eVentures	"To provide Deutsche Bank with partners in cutting edge technology and e-business solutions."	Deutsche Bank eVentures
Motorola	"To accelerate access to new technologies, new markets, and new talent."	One Motorola Ventures
Orange	"Gaining access to and accelerating the development of new technology companies."	Orange Ventures

Source: Company press releases and presentations

For companies it might be easiest to focus on creating value in the portfolio. As success in that case is based on a high IRR, success or failure can be easily measured in the short term. However, creating value for the parent company might sometimes not create the highest possible value in the portfolio in the short term and so could be ignored. Investment opportunities in companies that might help to ensure future revenue streams or might disrupt the business could be missed. Imagine where Ericsson would have been if it had not invested in Swedish Radio Systems, for example.

Corporate venture capital funds and "normal" VC funds differ in what makes them attractive from the start-up's perspective. As CVC and "normal" VC both have different added value to start-ups they often invest together. The VC focusing on its financial expertise and access to next rounds of financing and the CVC fund on its industry contacts, expertise and assets. Research has shown that start-ups rate CVC higher in terms of help with research and development, recruiting, international contacts, and setting up a sales infrastructure.[7] They benefit from the established company's tangible and intangible resources. However, "normal" VCs were preferred for support with getting additional rounds of financing and taking the company public. They can provide the financial knowledge that established companies may lack. However, an increasing number of established companies are structuring their CVC activities as a separate entity with people from outside with financial expertise.

As their offerings are so different, CVC funds and VC funds often invest together, combining their strengths. CVC funds tend not to take the lead with an investment and leave that to the VCs. Such collaborations appear to have been successful. However, as the market is getting tougher, conflicts arising from the different objectives, strategic versus IRR might be a challenge. The majority of the people running corporate venture capital activities at established companies are "first time" VCs and have only experienced the favorable economy of recent years.

An increasing number of established companies are structuring their CVC activities as a separate entity with people from outside with financial expertise.

TABLE 4.2 What CVC and "normal" VCs offer

CVC	"Normal" VC
Industry due diligence	Lead round (valuation)
Credibility – technical and commercial	Management support
Sales support, distribution channel	Executive recruitment
R&D support	Next rounds of financing
Possible trade sale	Support with IPO
Industry network/contacts	

Source: Interviews and powerpoint presentation, Berenschot (March 2000)

They have not been through the tougher times as we're having them now. Time will tell what happens.

Although many established companies missed out on the internet revolution, they seem intent on being part of the internet evolution. Corporate venture capital is a good way to see new webs of innovation emerge in the second act of the internet. Take for instance publishing giant Reed Elsevier. In 2000 it announced a $100 million venture fund that will invest on a global basis in e-businesses that could be of strategic interest to the company. This is a clear case of a company focusing on value creation for the parent company, using CVC as a way to see new webs of innovation arise.

As opposed to "normal" VC, corporate venture capital is not aimed at generating profits. There is often a strategic intent as well. The balance though differs per company. One could put CVC funds on a continuum with, on the one hand, a focus on value creation in the portfolio and on the other hand, value creation for the parent company. A focus on creation within the portfolio seems the most attractive as it is the easiest to measure and therefore to manage. It might create value for the company in the short term, although in the long term, creating value for the parent company is also important. However, the two aims are not mutually exclusive. Companies active in CVC should know where they are on the continuum though. For start-ups "normal" VCs and CVCs offer different things. Both VC financing and CVC financing have their advantages and to start-ups, as they are often complementary the two are often combined. Now let's discuss what makes corporate venture capital attractive to start-ups.

Why corporate venture capital appeals to start-ups

An increasing number of dot coms are finding out that a website is only a small part of the operation. Even more important is getting customers and making sure they stay. To get customers you need a well-known brand and credibility. That costs a lot of money. Even with a lot of money it's hard to build awareness and also make people buy stuff. It takes time as it is an organic process that you cannot accelerate. To make sure customers stay, you have to make sure you can deliver on what you promise. That means good fulfilment and distribution. A lot of companies are having a hard time doing that. Established companies have already been through that learning curve and have built the assets to do that. That's attractive to start-ups; a brand, customer base, distribution channel, experience, financial resources, and industry expertise. The established company could also be a potential lead customer.

Paul Gompers and Josh Lerner of the Harvard Business School found out that CVC has better results than "normal" VC.[8] This is especially true when there's a strategic fit. Also they usually pay more for their

Often it seems
companies invest
business related
their own VC
limited partner,
of innovation

that **established** ad-hoc in core start-ups, **via fund** or as a to see new webs grow.

shares than "normal" VCs. This is because plugging themselves into webs of innovation in an early stage is more important to them than getting a great deal.

A downside with CVC can be that the investing company is not well plugged into the financial community to assure next rounds. That is an aspect that start-ups often tend to forget, and often the enthusiasm that an established player wants to invest is dominating aspects like this. It can be compensated for by having a "normal" VC invest in that round as well. Another downside is that the established company might invest in, buy from, or acquire a competitor.

It seems as though established companies and start-ups have found each other. It's not about established companies against networks of start-ups but about these two groups working together in webs of innovation on the new, new thing. Each doing what they are best at – the start-up in building a new competence and the CVC in offering added value via things like its brand, distribution channel, and customer base. Corporate venture capital is one of the "glues" in the process from an established company's perspective.

As CVC is increasing certain patterns are emerging in how these activities are structured, although there is no single magic formula on how to organize CVC. The best way seems to differ in each organization, although a structured separate entity approach seems to have become increasingly popular. Let's have a closer look at these structures.

It comes in different flavours
Looking at patterns in how established companies are increasingly structuring their CVC activities I came across three ways of structuring CVC:

- ad hoc investments

- being a limited partner in funds managed by others

- having your own VC fund.

Of course there is flexibility and many companies combine these approaches. Sony for instance invests ad hoc via its business units, has several CVC funds and is a limited partner in some funds. Often it seems that established companies invest ad hoc in core business related start-ups and via their own VC fund or as a limited partner to see new webs of innovation coming up, or creating them to ensure future growth. Combinations are also evident. As discussed later in this chapter, an increasing number of companies with their own VC fund are allowing external limited partners as Intel did with its Intel 64 fund.

By "ad hoc investments" I mean doing investments ad hoc via the business units or via functional departments such as the finance department. Investments are made because that is wanted at the time. This is not a structured approach. This approach is often chosen with a strategic intent; to stay in touch with the market and the opportunity for buying more shares later or even acquiring. IBM is one company that is doing it this way.

As the aim is clearly to create value for the parent company and is done by parts of the organization that know exactly what the need is to improve existing business it is made certain that there is a strategic alignment. While this is an advantage of ad hoc investments there is always the potential of internal political twist to it; other parts of the organization might perceive the investment as a threat that could cannibalize their activities. Or this could slow down investments decisions or they might try to slowdown investment decisions because of other internal rivalries going on. This in general can be a problem with established companies when doing ad hoc investments; not being able to decide with speed. Quite often within this CVC structure the "go" or "no go" decision is taken by the executive management team of the company. When there are other priorities the go or no go decision can take a while.

Besides potential cannibalization by the investment or internal rivalries, another thing that affects the speed of the decision process is the fear of failure. Having failures in a portfolio is normal. Silicon Valley VCs have a success ratio of 1 in 20. If failure or decline in potential is likely, they get out of the company. At a workshop on corporate venture capital it turned out that this is one of the major problems of companies doing ad hoc investments; getting out on time when needed. As the investment is done under the brand of the established company it is afraid of damage to the brand, so they tend to stick longer to an investment in the hope that it will improve. VCs know better when to leave a sinking ship. Companies fear failures that might damage their brand and can therefore be slow in their decisions. They're dealing with the fear versus greed dilemma; a fear to make an investment that fails versus greed to not miss out on the right investments because of the value creation they could bring.

So the threat of slow decision making is a disadvantage of ad hoc investments. Another one is that once the investment is made some established companies tend to want to have too much control and get involved too much. As an American former executive of the Silicon Valley subsidiary of one of the largest European TMT companies told me: "VC is like a horse race: know the track, know the horse, know the jockey and place your bet. But don't send a committee out to ride the horse!"

Established company bureaucratic thinking can frustrate the entrepreneurial mindset in a start-up, and can eventually kill immature start-ups. It can also kill talented management. The high profile Silicon Valley executive quoted above left the organization to join a high profile start-up in the Valley.

This brings me to another problem, that of internal employee dynamics. In established companies it is quite normal for people to change jobs within the organization, get promoted or leave the organization. This can kill the relationship, as these relations are often people based. With reorganizations, some investments might be dropped to save costs or because they are perceived not to be of any strategic interest anymore. The larger the company, the weirder the reasoning can sometimes seem. All of these things can lead to cutting the ties which might have huge implications for the start-up's image. Scenarios for these cases are increasingly put on paper before any investments are made to protect both parties.

Often when doing ad hoc investments they are done as a side dish by somebody. This has two disadvantages. The first is that this person can be forced to spend less time on the venture by higher management. The second disadvantage is the potential lack of experience/expertise as he or she usually is not an experienced investor/investment manager. All of this can slow down or block the whole process of investing. Therefore companies often outsource the closing of the deal to investment banks or other companies, which only solves the problem of closing the deal. That's just the beginning of the relationship. The real work starts with adding the value the established company has to offer and assuring next rounds of financing, which is often underestimated as I found out during a workshop on the subject.

One advantage is the fact that are made brand of

to this option
investments
under the
the venture
capital fund.

Besides ad hoc investments, established companies also invest as limited partners alongside similar companies and institutional investors in a fund managed by others. An example is Accel Partners' Internet Technology Fund II in 1998 that has investors like Lucent, Microsoft, Compaq Computer, and Nortel. Global chemicals and plastics company Dow Chemical is a limited partner in about 20 funds (December 2000).

There are two major advantages to this option. First, the fact that investments are made under the brand of the venture capital fund. If the investments fail, this does not directly damage the limited partners' brand. Second, sharing the risks of the investments with other investors. This may also be a disadvantage as conflicts of interest can arise among the limited partners. The limited partners might have different objectives with the investments and might compete at some stage for acquisitions, etc.

Besides conflicts of interest between limited partners there's also the difference between the objectives of the partners of the fund and the limited partners. The partners of the fund are only driven by getting a management fee (percentage of the funds managed) and carry (percentage of the profits) that are as high as possible and are less concerned about the strategic aspects. That's all right when the focus is on creating value within the portfolio but not if the focus is on creating value within the parent company.

Limited partners are limited in what they can do. They are limited in their control over the fund, and this is often hard for established companies that are used to management by control. Part of the limitation is the restricted access to the portfolio of the VC fund. Each fund differs as to what extent investors can participate in the whole process of selecting potential investees, deciding on whether or not to invest, making the investment and helping the company to become successful. Often there is a relation between the extent to which limited partners want to participate in the whole process and the intent of their CVC activities. When the intent of the limited partners is to create value in the portfolio the need is probably less than when the intent is to create value in the parent company.

Besides ad hoc investments and being a limited partner a structure that seems to increase in popularity is for a company to have its own VC fund. With this option the CVC activities are set up using a VC fund that is a separate legal entity as a vehicle for the CVC activities. It is usually set up as an autonomous partnership structure. Allthough the majority of these funds seem to be set up in the past few years the amounts invested and the number of investments are impressive. Table 4.3 provides some examples of the figures involved.

TABLE 4.3 Autonomous CVC funds

Company	Fund name	Since	Amount invested ($m)	Number of companies in portfolio
Dell	Dell Venture	1999	800	90
Siemens	Mustang Ventures	1998	200	18
Sun	Sun Venture and Strategic Investment Fund	1999	500	40

Source: several articles and corporate press releases published between January and September 2000

The fact of having the CVC activities separated from the rest of the organization is the major advantage. Because of the autonomy the fund can operate as flexibly as its "normal" VC counterparts on making investment decisions, exiting or, if necessary, liquidating businesses. All of this without office politics. As employees of the partnership are entirely involved with existing investments and making new investments, investments are more professionally managed. The other advantage of having this knowledge in house is that it ensures being in full control of the investments.

From an accounting perspective the advantage of this autonomy is that it has the benefit of profits when any are made and it does not have to declare losses that occur in between from less successful investments.

Of course, there are also disadvantages. It is difficult to attract and retain good venture capital employees. If they're not incentivized they leave. It differs among companies how employees are incentivized. But even when properly compensated, there remains the risk that employees will leave to either set up their own fund or join a "normal" fund. That is dangerous as investing is a people-based activity; it's all about personal relations. If employees leave that does not improve the business.

When the focus of the fund is creating value for the parent company the threat arises of lack of strategic alignment. As the fund is loosely connected to the parent company there is less insight into strategic alignment in terms of what has already been developed in house, what can be acquired and what should be invested in. In other words looking for an investment focus; an analysis of the "white spaces" in the organization, the needs. After investments are made it really starts though – getting buy-in and support from existing businesses in order to deliver on the CVC added value proposition. While this might be challenging when the fund is loosely connected to the rest of the organization, it might end up being seen by the rest of the company as a peripheral activity. Reuters is an example of a company that is very aware of that. Its Greenhouse fund has a chief marketing officer whose role it is to scan both the portfolio and the needs in the company to make matches where possible. The Greenhouse funds also organizes informal events to stimulate networking between its portfolio and the existing lines of business. The fund sometimes invites senior management to visit places like Silicon Valley to listen to 25-minute pitches by portfolio companies, with the objective of making these executives aware of the existence of these companies with the goal of getting support and having potential customers. Other options I learned of during my research are involving the existing businesses in the due diligence process or having existing business managers on the board of a venture. The latter can often be part of some kind of "adoption" or sponsoring of a venture by a business unit.

Table 4.4 provides a summary of the options and their advantages and disadvantages.

When the executive management team does not see the importance of CVC, the initiative is highly likely to fail, according to one former executive of an established company. He suggested that acknowledging the importance of CVC should be linked to a clear focus on either portfolio value creation or being parent company value driven. If it is parent company value driven the goal should be to use for instance at least two products from the portfolio of companies a year. When it is portfolio value creation driven the goal should be to establish a definite ROI figure every year.

TABLE 4.4 Pros and cons of CVC options

Option	Pros	Cons
Ad hoc	Potential strategic alignment	• The threat of strategic conflict • Potential brand damage • Threat of slow decision process • Lack of investing expertise
Own VC firm	• Total control • Flexibility • In between losses don't have to be declared	• Attracting and retaining good VCs • Potential brand damage • Threat of lack of strategic alignment
Limited partner	• Spread of risks • Brand protection	• Restricted access to portfolio company management • Conflicts of interest

When the emphasis is on creating value for the parent company a good link between the fund management and the rest of the company seems to be key. That is why the CVC funds are usually run by people who used to have senior positions in the company. The general partner of Lucent's Lucent Venture Partners, John Hanley, used to be the company's vice president of strategy. Also these managers tend to be intrapreneurial types; on the one hand able to deal with company politics and on the other hand able to deal with CVC dynamics.

Many companies setting up CVC activities are struggling with how to do it. Consider incentives, for example. Talented VCs come at a cost. Usually at "normal" VC funds, an annual management fee is paid in addition to salary and a carry (about 20–30 percent of the profits

When the emphasis is on creating value for the parent company a **good link** between the fund management and the rest of the company **seems to be key.**

made). This can lead to people working on CVC making more money than their counterparts in the rest of the organizations. The Xerox Technology Ventures $30 million fund generated an estimated $219 million. Of that total an estimated $175 million was for Xerox and the remaining $44 million for the three remaining partners.[10] These type of numbers can lead to jealousy. On the other hand, not rewarding according to market standards leads to the problem of not attracting, or not retaining talented people, a dilemma faced by many companies. They often try to solve it by having the CVC activities in a separate legal entity where it is easier to offer market-conforming incentives as they are isolated from the rest of the organization.

As established companies are increasingly active in CVC in an attempt to make sure they do not miss out on new webs of innovation to ensure future growth and strategic renewal in the internet evolution, they're also increasingly structuring these activities. There is no one perfect format as all structures have their advantages and disadvantages, and a combination of the structures is usually chosen. Let's have a look at the approach of cell phone manufacturer Nokia.

Nokia Venture Partners
In April 1998 Nokia launched its Nokia Venture Partners fund with $100 million. Acknowledging the importance of networked innovation for strategic renewal the CEO,

CFO, and President appointed then vice president of business development for Nokia Americas, John Malloy, to set up the operations.

The fund operates as an autonomous partnership. It has its own supervisory board in which representatives of the limited partners take place. The latest fund includes external limited partners as well. Nokia is nevertheless still the significant limited partner.

The overall structure of Nokia is composed of four business units: Nokia Mobile Phones, Nokia Networks, Nokia Research Center, and the Nokia Venture Organization. The latter unit comprises the majority of the networked innovation related activities. The two business units Nokia Mobile Phones and Nokia Networks leverage and expand the existing business. Nokia's Research Center explores new technologies in a classical research and development approach. For internal ideas that do not fit within the existing businesses Nokia has an internal venturing program called the Entrepreneurial Web. Nokia has defined three new business areas: Nokia Internet Communications, Nokia Home Communications, and Nokia Mobile Display Appliances that are explored and developed by these ventures. Nokia Venture Partners complements the organization by investing independently in external ventures in the mobile internet to keep in touch with new webs of innovation.

The fund focuses on ventures in the mobile internet field. It excludes companies that might be in direct conflict with Nokia's current businesses from the outset. Furthermore its investment criteria do not differ from "normal" venture capital funds; potential for a significant market, a strong management team with execution capacities and defendable barriers to market. Nokia Venture Partners typically takes the lead in investments and sits on boards. So far the fund has invested in 26 companies (February 2001).

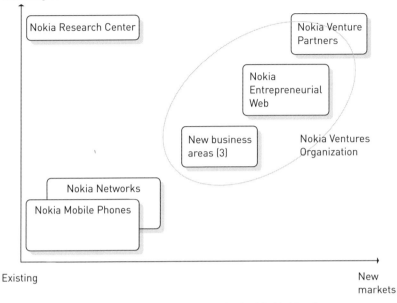

New
technologies

Nokia Research Center

Nokia Venture
Partners

Nokia
Entrepreneurial
Web

New business
areas (3)

Nokia Ventures
Organization

Nokia Networks

Nokia Mobile Phones

Existing

New
markets

FIGURE 4.4 Nokia Ventures Organization in the big Nokia picture

Its five partners decide on investment decisions on a day-to-day basis.
The supervisory board supervises the "big picture" on behalf of all
limited partners. All of the partners have a (senior) background at
Nokia. Their functional backgrounds are R&D, accounting, legal, and
marketing/operational. All of them have deal-making experience
(usually in the field of mergers and acquisitions). The five partners
supervise about ten investment professionals with different
backgrounds, most of them not from Nokia.

The fact that the five partners all have a senior background is key as this
gives them credit within the existing businesses and makes sure they
know their way around within the companies informal networks. For
companies with autonomous partnerships, finding support for the

"If you only strategic having an IRR may end up the fund investing in that are not invest for reasons without discipline you compromising profitability by technologies viable."

ventures with the existing business can sometimes be challenging – having partners that know the parent organization makes a big difference. Nevertheless this can sometimes still remain a challenge such as when a business unit feels threatened by a venture, for example.

As the fund has only been around since 1998 it is too early to judge performance. So far there have been a number of trade sales with good returns on investment but there have been no public offerings yet. Nokia has not acquired any of the portfolio companies. It does not intend to do so but will not exclude the option. The objective is to outperform the market (usually an IRR of 20–30 percent). Speaking with the partners the strong emphasis on IRR was apparent. Several times the partners clearly stated that Nokia Venture Partners does not invest for strategic reasons. In their opinion, the only way to be successful is to focus on IRR. "If you only invest for strategic reasons without having an IRR discipline you may end up compromising the fund profitability by investing in technologies that are not viable," one of the partners told me. To encourage the IRR focus its employees are incentivized according to market norms. This is also to retain employees as knowledge of the wireless market is a wanted skill in the venture capital market these days.

Nokia Venture Partners started in 1998 in Menlo Park, Helsinki and Washington DC in the US and in 1999 its European office in London was opened. The organization plans to start operations in Asia in 2001. In 1998 the fund started with $100 million, later increased to $150 million with Nokia as the only limited partner. As more capital was needed a new fund was raised in 2000, this time for $500 million and also including other limited partners such as Goldman Sachs, BMC Software, CDB Webtech, and others. The need for capital was of course a driver for this but other advantages were added value provided by these limited partners and it is an extra way to drive the IRR focus.

With both expansion in terms of the size of the fund and geographic expansion the challenge for the fund is to manage the growth. Over time the performance of the portfolio will show how successful Nokia Venture Partners has been.

The future
Looking at the patterns in the way established companies structure their CVC activities I saw an interesting development emerging; companies with their own venture capital funds allowing other limited partners. Table 4.6 contains examples of the CVC funds with their external limited partners.

On the surface the obvious reasons are that this provides them with capital and reduces the risk, in addition to the added value in terms of expertise, network, or assets. This is the case for the established company that sets up the fund. The limited partners are often established companies. Investing in the VC funds of other established companies allows them to learn from how these companies are plugging themselves into webs of innovation and also becoming parts of these webs of innovation. When the intent of all participants is value creation for the parent company, this might be a better way to do it than by being a limited partner in a "normal" VC fund because in these funds the aim of the partners is value creation in the portfolio. Time will reveal how this development has worked out for both the companies that have set up these funds and the limited partners.

In the more mature American market the number of companies with their own CVC company is larger than in the less mature European market.[10] As the US market led the way earlier for CVC one could therefore state that companies will move towards the autonomous partnership model as CVC matures.

TABLE 4.5 CVC funds with their external limited partners

Company name	Fund name	Since	Fund size ($m)	Outside limited partners
Ericsson	Ericsson Venture Fund	2000	300	Merill Lynch, Investor AB, Industrivarden
Intel	Intel 64 Fund	1999	300	Compaq, Dell, Hewlett-Packard, Intel, NEC, SGI, Bank of America, The Boeing Company, Circuit City, Enron, Ford Motor Company, General Electric, McKessonHBOC, Morgan Stanley Dean Witter, Reuters, Sabre, SmithKline Beecham, Sumitomo Corporation, SunAmerica, and Telmex
Nokia	Nokia Venture Partners	2000	500	Goldman Sachs, BMC Software, CDBWebTech, and others

Sources: Ericsson.com, Intel64fund.com, Nokiaventurepartners.com

CVC activities seem to be increasingly structured as CVC is maturing. General Electric for example has been active for about 20–25 years in CVC but formally structured the operations in 1994 in the US and 1995 in Europe, when it formed GE Equity. Nowadays it invests $1 billion globally per year. One of the directors of the company told me that the goal is creating value in the portfolio and therefore a link with one of GE's businesses is not needed. It has had successes in its portfolio, such as iMediation, an e-commerce infrastructure software and services company, for example.

Part of the structuring is that companies are trying to standardize the decision-making process around investments. Many funds spent so much time on raising their funds internally and doing their PR that they did not spend too much time on thinking about how to select and decide on investments and manage a portfolio. CVC managers are finding that it is hard to standardize and/or scale operations. A director active in CVC for an established American high tech company told me that they had achieved a reduction in the number of days needed to make an investment decision from 60 to 25 in about a year by using automated tools to file business plans, create the knowledge database, and to define the assessment process. However he stressed that it still remains a human task; personal knowledge and skills are required, which are hard to transfer.

CVC is a people's business that is not standardizable and scalable. That is the threat when employees are not retained; that as soon as they walk out the door they take all the knowledge and skills with them. As venture capital funds often approach CVC employees with attractive options this is a serious threat to established companies active in CVC. Most CVC managers do not perceive this as a threat as they reward their employees well. However, there are plenty of examples in the market of VCs with well-known funds that used to work for established

Corporate
is **one of the**
of networked
is becoming

venture capital

key components

innovation and

increasingly

structured.

companies in the CVC business. One of the partners at Silicon Valley based Bowman Capital for instance worked for five years for Intel Capital.[12]

However, as employees for CVC activities are concerned, "normal" VC funds were especially attractive during the internet revolution when enormous amounts of money were made thanks to the outrageous valuations and relatively short path from idea to IPO. Success seemed to be guaranteed for VCs. Now the hype is over though, as I argued in Chapter 2. Future success will be difficult.

One thing is clear. Since the arrival of the internet CVC is becoming increasingly popular as established companies are acknowledging the importance of CVC as one of the key components of networked innovation helping established companies to see new webs of innovation come up to ensure future growth and strategic renewal in the internet evolution. As CVC matures it seems that setting up autonomous partnerships is the preferred structure. Inviting outside limited partners seems to be a new trend.

Conclusion

Corporate venture capital is one of the key components of networked innovation and is becoming increasingly structured. It differs from "normal" VCs in that there are more objectives than making a lot of money. These objectives differ for each company and can be put on a continuum, on the one hand creating value in the portfolio and on the other hand creating value in the parent company. Companies should be aware where their CVC activities are on that continuum. It might be the easiest to focus on value creation in the portfolio. Although this can create significant value in the mid to long term this might result in companies missing out on creating value in the parent company for strategic renewal in the long term and ensuring future growth in the internet evolution. Via

CVC, companies can invest in start-ups that they might end up acquiring. It seems that the autonomous partnership is the preferred structure. There is a trend towards inviting external limited partners to join funds.

So far we have talked about two key components of networked innovation; internal venturing and corporate venture capital. As these two options are often in an early stage, there might be occasions when a company is just too late and a start-up has already developed some interesting offerings. Then acquisition might be the best option to cheaply acquire competences. This is the subject of Chapter 5.

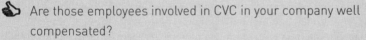

Key points

 Does your company invest in start-ups in a structured way? If so, what type out of the three described and what is the logic behind it? How would another structure fit? Or a combination?

 How do you measure and motivate value creation for the parent company?

Are those employees involved in CVC in your company well compensated?

How is success with CVC measured within your company – by value creation in the portfolio or in the parent company?

 What are your company's investment criteria?

How long does the investment process take for investments within your company and how do you think this process could be shortened?

What are the barriers to succesful CVC?

 How do you ensure support from the existing business?

 What do ventures want and how can companies active in CVC add value to these ventures?

 Does the management team acknowledge the importance of CVC?

 What is the return on investment on CVC within your company?

 How do you convince top management of the importance of CVC?

 Does CVC compete with "normal" VC or do they complement each other?

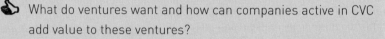 How are the right connections made between your CVC portfolio companies and the lines of business?

Would it be interesting for your CVC fund to have external limited partners?

Further information

At the website **www.websofinnovation.com** you can find additional resources on the subject, such as links to relevant articles, books, websites and over time this will be expanded. A mailing list on the subject of this chapter allows you to discuss it with other readers.

Notes

1. Gompers, Paul and Lerner, Josh. "The determinants of corporate venture capital success: organizational structure, incentives, and complementarities," working paper 6725, Cambridge, National Bureau of Economic Research 1998.

2. Berenschot. "Corporate Venturing wordt in Europa nog weinig toegepast, maar heeft veel potentie," presentation, Utrecht, March 2000.

3. Ericsson.com.

4. Moss Kanter, Rosabeth. *Evolve!*, Harvard Business School Press, Boston, MA 2001.

5. Williams, Molly. "Corporate Venture Capital Cools Off," *Wall Street Journal Europe*, July 5, 2001.

6. "Corporate venturing in Europe," Enterprise Directorate-General of the European Commission, Innovation Policy Unit 2000.

7. Berenschot. "Corporate Venturing wordt in Europa nog weinig toegepast, maar heeft veel potentie," presentation, Utrecht, March 2000.

8. Gompers, Paul and Lerner, Josh. Op. cit.

9. Gompers, Paul and Lerner, Josh. Op. cit.

10. Enterprise Directorate-General, Innovation Policy Unit. Op. cit.

11. "Corporate VC arms can't pin down talent," Redherring.com, November 28, 2000.

five

[acquire and develop]

HAVE YOU EVER HEARD OF HOTMAIL? DO YOU USE IT, OR KNOW anybody who uses the free e-mail service? You probably do. Hotmail is one of the fastest growing consumer services on the internet to date. It grew in a few years from 100 users in the first hour in 1996 to about 70 million active users worldwide in 2000.

When you think of Hotmail you think of MSN (Microsoft Network). That's not without reason as it is a service offered by Microsoft under the MSN umbrella. But the interesting thing is that the company wasn't started by Microsoft. It was started by an Indian-born engineer called Sabeer Bhatia. At the time no other similar service was offered. He created the company and grew it until in 1997 his company was acquired by Microsoft for $400 million when it had about 10 million users. From there on Microsoft grew the company further to its current status. It is one of the most visited domains owned by the company.

In the eighties associated with for their or technologies. that started to acquiring order to get

acquisitions were
buying companies
production plants
In the nineties
change towards
companies in
brains and new
products in house.

Acquisitions is one of the other key components of networked innovation. It can be a second phase after having invested in a company via CVC or done because certain competences are missing in-house. Acquisitions seem to increase in popularity and the reasoning behind it seems to change as well.

In the eighties acquisitions were associated with buying companies for their production plants or technologies. In the nineties that started to change towards acquiring companies in order to get brains and new products in house. As this practice is maturing, companies are increasingly seeing acquisitions as a way to buy themselves into new webs of innovation.

After the hype, many companies have found that building a profitable and sustainable business is hard and are looking for an established company to acquire them, thus leveraging the assets of the acquiring company. For the acquiring company it is a way to help them become dot corps by leveraging the technology, and front and back office functions developed by the start-up and also to get access to the web of innovation of which the start-up is part.

Acquisitions have become a way of getting competences within the company. In Silicon Valley people already talk about "A&D", or acquire and develop. This allows both start-ups and established companies to do what they are good at. The start-ups creating businesses out of new concepts and established companies acquiring them and developing them further by using their customers and so on. Acquisitions as a way into webs of innovation. Established companies and start-ups working together instead of against each other to help established companies become dot corps in the internet evolution.

Acquiring companies is hard though. It seems companies are increasingly structuring their acquisition strategy to better deal with them. As a best practices example we will have a look at Cisco, a company with a structured approach towards acquisitions.

An increasing number of acquisitions

As many start-ups are struggling to survive they become a target for established companies. Especially since the market correction in 1999 these start-ups have become a cheap way for established companies to buy brains and bring new products in house. Valuations of these start-ups dropped drastically, sometimes more than 50 percent. Even some companies that were predicted to make established players become obsolete not too long ago got acquired as they were struggling to survive. Online CD retailer Cdnow was acquired by media giant Bertelsmann and online supermarket Peapod by grocery giant Ahold.

The current consolidation in the market also stimulates acquisitions among the dot coms. The larger fish buying the smaller ones or the smaller ones joining forces. Table 5.1 provides a few examples of acquisitions carried out in early 2001. It is interesting to note that none of these companies, buyers or sellers, is profitable.

During the hype, start-ups floated sometimes only a few months after being founded. Online grocer Webvan for instance went public three months after it started. This whole craze is changing. The stock

TABLE 5.1 The larger fish buying the smaller fish

Acquiring company	Acquired company
AmericanGreetings.com	Egreetings network
Dietwatch.com	Cyberdiet.com
Ivillage	Women.com

Source: **www.thestandard.com/article/display/0,1151, 22291,00**

exchanges are also waking up and increasingly applying old economy criteria to "new" economy companies. The IPO used to be a way to get financing for start-ups. But the path to flotation is becoming longer and not that obvious. A good alternative is acquisitions. In Silicon Valley a company called Webmergers.com provides a research-backed hub for buyers and sellers of internet properties. It also maintains a database of mergers and acquisitions involving internet destinations. As you can see in Figure 5.1, the number of internet-related M&A deals is increasing significantly, as are the amounts spent on them per year (from $8.4 billion in 1998 to $87.3 billion in 2000).

Silicon Valley is often ahead of the rest of the world in ICT trends. Whereas it used to be that people were starting a company in the

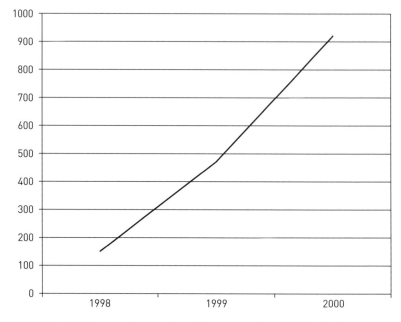

FIGURE 5.1 An increasing number of internet-related M&A deals

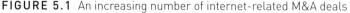

Source: Webmergers.com, excluding the AOL/TimeWarner deal, because its size would distort the trend

Valley to become the next Cisco or eBay that is changing towards building their companies to be bought by the latter and further grown, leveraging the tangible and intangible assets of the established company such as brand, expertise, and distribution channel. It can also give credibility to potential customers if you are part of an established firm.

Top VCs in Silicon Valley are increasingly building companies with the goal of having it acquired. In this way VCs will become off income statement R&D for established companies.[1] An example is Cerent. Partner Vinod Khosla at the well-known Silicon Valley based VC firm Kleiner Perkins Caufield & Byers, perceived the need to make the rings of fiber-optic cables that encircle many metropolitan areas more efficient, in 1996. He recruited the first employees and served as chief executive for 18 months, after that as chairman and his VC firm invested $8 million in the company for a 30 percent stake. From there on it grew quickly and in 1999 the company was acquired by Cisco for $6.9 billion.[2]

Acquisition used to be second choice. If you were acquired you were a loser; you were not good enough for public flotation. The winning companies went public. But as the internet hype is over it is becoming a respected exit strategy. During the internet revolution the thinking was that start-ups were all created with the objective of making established companies become obsolete. A David versus Goliath feeling predominated. This is however changing, as the companies that were supposed to make the established companies become obsolete are struggling to survive it becomes clear that in the internet evolution, start-ups are created to help established companies become dot corps. Instead of a David versus Goliath relationship it becomes Davids and Goliaths both doing what they're best at. The start-up creates something new, quickly and the established company acquires it and grows it into a large business by doing what it's good at; making and selling a lot of products. Entrepreneurs are now starting companies with the objective of being acquired by established companies, not to let them become obsolete. David and Goliath working on the new, new thing in webs of innovation.

Being acquired used to be seen as losing. However, now that the hype is over and start-ups are finding out that it is difficult to build a profitable and sustainable business, being acquired by an established company is an attractive option because of the tangible and intangible assets offered. Start-ups are even set up with the purpose of being acquired. For established companies this is a way to cheaply acquire competences that they can further develop in-house and has the potential to increase revenues.

Getting brains and new products
Whereas in the eighties the objective of an acquisition was to buy production plants or technologies, in the nineties the objective is rather to obtain intellectual assets such as talent that is experienced in a certain technology or market, technological innovation, a customer base, and next generation products.

In the eighties there was an industrial approach towards acquisitions because of the assumptions made. "Eighties style" assumptions were that companies consist of operational parts that are worth more apart than together. In this model, employees were just production assets as machines were. All these assets were assumed to be valued objectively.

These assumptions began to change in the nineties. The importance of "soft assets" such as talent, technological innovation, a company's web of innovation and customer base were increasingly acknowledged. These were all things that were hard to quantify. However, everybody agreed that if these assets were of good quality they could bring in significant future revenue streams, so acquiring companies were willing to pay huge amounts to acquire companies with the right soft assets. If you look at what the acquiring party gets in return; intellectual assets like talent, technological innovation, a customer base, and a next generation of products, you can understand the price. You pay for the intangible assets to keep up in an increasingly fast-changing business. AOL for instance paid $300 million to acquire Mirabilis (the company behind ICQ). For that amount they got the technological innovation ICQ and the customer base. It is estimated that there are 20 million active users.

Established companies are increasingly becoming aware that start-ups are sometimes simply better at networked innovation. Instead of letting a start-up become a competitor, the best option is to buy and further develop it. This offers the company direct access to the web of innovation that the start-up is part of. With the acquisition of internet-related companies, the established companies aim to kick start their internet competence instead of reinventing the wheel themselves as things go too fast to develop themselves. As the valuation craze is over

Established companies are **increasingly becoming aware** that start-ups are sometimes **simply better at networked innovation.** Instead of letting a start-up become a competitor, the best option is to **buy and further develop it.**

the companies have also become cheaper. In 2000 Bertelsmann acquired CDnow for $3 a share. This was roughly one-fifth of the share price at which it floated in 1998. Acquisitions are therefore a cheap way to acquire competences for established companies to become dot corps.

An example of an acquisition of an established company because of getting next generation products in-house is Intel's acquisition of Level One. Intel has realized that its focus on the desktop is insufficient because in the near future, computers are likely to get much of their processing power from networks. Most of the growth and margins in Intel's business will come from networking equipment. To extend its semiconductor expertise from PCs, Intel acquired Level One, a company that makes silicon building blocks for high-speed connectivity.[3] Since 1999, Intel has spent about $10.3 billion on acquiring some 36 communications companies.[4]

Unfortunately acquiring companies is not easy, as many companies find out. Signing the papers and transferring money and stocks is only the beginning. It must then be decided whether to leave the company to act autonomously, integrate it with a certain line of business or whatever structural solution. Key employees might decide to leave or there might be some weaknesses in the acquired company you were not aware of.

It is hard to find the right balance between telling the acquired companies what you want and letting them act as a start-up from an established company's perspective. I have heard many stories of start-ups that became frustrated by the established company's need for control and for things to be done the "company way" after their acquisition by an established company. This is one reason why companies are structuring their acquisition activities and dedicating resources. Acquiring companies and making them fit with your business is a discipline in itself. After a few years you can measure how well the acquisition worked out by looking at the value generation by the acquired company and the percentage of employees who resign. As you will read later in this chapter, Cisco has a very structured approach to acquisitions with dedicated teams and standardized procedures. It clearly pays off as about 40 percent of Cisco's revenues originate from acquired competences.[5]

From an established company perspective another factor is also important, i.e. that acquisitions are usually cash and equity deals. In exchange for the company the shareholders are paid partly in cash and partly in shares of the acquiring company. When the shares are performing poorly this is not a good proposition. A practical problem can be that there are not enough shares available. Then an issue has to be made in order to have enough shares to pay. This is not something a company does easily and is not often preferred by the shareholders. Nevertheless this does not seem to prevent established companies from acquiring dot coms, as evidenced by the growing number of internet-related acquisitions.

In the past acquisitions used to be an ad hoc activity but this is changing. An increasing number of companies acknowledge the importance of doing acquisitions well by starting, standardizing, and structuring their acquisition activities. They see the importance of acquisitions as one of the key components of networked innovation as established companies are trying to plug themselves into webs of innovation to become dot corps.

Cisco is well known for its successful and well-structured approach. Below is an in-depth look at their approach.

Another

there must be

the acquisition

term for the

makes them

they are one of

acquiring the

criterion is that something in in the short employees that want to stay, as the reasons for company.

Cisco: Silicon Valley as its lab

Cisco has increased the number of acquisitions as shown in Figure 5.2. In 2000 Cisco acquired 23 companies. Cisco does almost no R&D itself anymore and is known for its well-structured acquisition policy. Some say it has replaced its R&D department by an A&D (Acquire and Develop) department. About 40 percent of Cisco's $5 billion revenues originate from the products of companies that it acquired.[6] The company acknowledges that sometimes it misses out on webs of innovation, and more importantly, that start-ups are better at creating new competences. Through acquisitions the company can make sure it plugs itself into the relevant webs of innovation.

Thanks to its structured approach it can be fast and successful in its acquisitions. Not all of the acquisitions have been successful, although the majority have been. Its first acquisition Crescendo, bought in 1993 by Cisco for $89 million generates about $4 billion in revenue annually.[7]

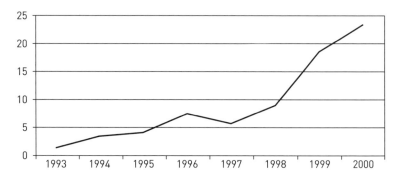

FIGURE 5.2 Cisco's acquisitions 1993–2000

Source: Cisco.com

The CEO formally approves all deals but is only actively involved with the major ones. Cisco has a team that continuously monitors the market for upcoming webs of innovation. An additional advantage of this is that by separating these activities the company knows what's going on in the market, what's worked on internally, and when external companies do things better, cheaper, or faster they can be acquired. Sometimes the company decides to wait and take a minority stake instead of acquiring.

Cisco's customers also drive the company's acquisition policy. The customer US West for instance, was a driving factor behind the decision in March 1998 to acquire NetSpeed, which manufactures equipment that turns regular phone lines into high-speed digital subscriber line (DSL) data conduits.[8]

Part of Cisco's structured approach to acquisitions are the criteria it uses. Cisco has developed some very clear criteria for acquisitions. One of the first things it wants to find out is whether there is a shared vision; both on the future of the industry and the technology. Which players will play which roles and how the technology will develop over time. Another criterion is that there must be something in the acquisition in the short term for the employees that makes them want to stay, as they are one of the reasons for acquiring the company. In the long term there should be something in it for the shareholders, employees, customers, and business partners. The company's long-term strategy should match Cisco's. Last but not least is that there should be a chemistry between the acquired company and Cisco; the cultures have to be similar, otherwise integration will not be feasible.[9] Physical proximity used to be another criterion. Thanks to the ease of online communications, the company has been able to broaden its sights and successfully integrate companies from throughout the US and the rest of the world.[10]

Cisco has been

and most clear

the move from

For Cisco

having

Valley

one of the first **examples** of R&D to A&D. that means **Silicon** as its lab.

Once the companies are acquired a structured process takes off. The minute an acquisition deal is signed specialized integration teams take care of integrating the acquired companies. These usually operate quickly as during the whole process prior to acquisition, the teams have already looked at aspects such as financial and human resources so they know what to do when the deal is signed. Cisco's policy is usually to integrate the company as a business unit in charge of its own product engineering and marketing but the acquired company's sales and manufacturing are centralized.

Usually the acquisition is mainly paid for with options in Cisco. This has generally been a strong share, which makes it an attractive proposition to potential acquisition targets.

In an interview Cisco's CEO and President John Chambers describes the acquisition strategy the best when he states: "Our ideal acquisition is a small start-up that has a great technology product on the drawing board that is going to come out in 6–12 months. We buy the engineers and the next generation product. Then we blow it through our distribution channels and leverage our manufacturing and financial strengths."[11]

The question must be asked how Cisco's acquisitions will go if its stock continues to be valued low as it is right now. Cisco's share was at $82 in April 2000 and a year later in April 2001 it was at $14. As this is the main currency it pays its acquired companies in, this could have a major impact as a poorly performing stock is a better proposition in an offer than a poorly performing stock.

However, Cisco has been one of the first and most clear examples of the move from R&D to A&D. For Cisco that means having Silicon Valley as its lab.

Conclusion

Acquisitions used to be made in order to acquire tangible assets but the focus is now shifting towards intangible assets, such as brains and next generation products. In other words, acquisitions are being seen as a way to get into webs of innovation, as one of the key components of networked innovation. For start-ups it's becoming an accepted exit strategy. Some start-ups are even building their business with the aim of having it acquired.

Acquiring companies is not easy though. Companies such as Cisco acknowledge this by having a structured and standardized process with clear acquisition criteria, dedicated teams for integrating the acquired companies, and so on.

Now we've been through why large companies are having such a hard time dealing with disruptive technologies, the most recent one being the internet. Established companies missed out in the internet revolution and therefore want to make sure they do not miss out in the internet evolution by plugging themselves into webs of innovation. They do this through a combination of internal venturing, corporate venture capital, and acquisitions. But how to structure for networked innovation? That's the subject for Chapter 6, which discusses how companies are dealing with this and shows that some companies are even creating nodes of networked innovation to facilitate networked innovation as they move towards becoming dot corps.

Key points

👍 Does your company have a structured acquisition policy? If so, compare it with Cisco's.

▶

Think of acquisitions you were either involved in or heard about; what's the situation now? How has it created any value for the company?

 Would you know of any companies that would be interesting to acquire?

If your company has acquired companies in the past, what percentage of the acquired company's employees stayed?

Does your company hold any stakes in start-ups that might be worth acquiring?

Further information

At the website **www.websofinnovation.com** you can find additional resources on the subject, such as links to relevant articles, books, websites and this will be expanded over time. A mailing list on the subject of this chapter allows you to discuss it with other readers.

Notes

1. Hansell, Saul. "Now that we're still here, where do we go? Seven answers," *New York Times*, February 28, 2001.

2. "Cisco buys Khosla's Cerent for $6.9 bn," on indian-express.com, Indian Express Newspapers Ltd, Bombay, September 4, 2000.

3. Chauduri and Tabrizi, 1999.

4. Goodin, Dan. "Intel's Barret Vow to Continue Communications Buying Spree, *Wall Street Journal Europe*, May 9, 2001.

5. Shinal, John. "Can Mike Volpi make Cisco sizzle again?" *Business Week*, McGraw Hill Group, New York NY, February 26, 2001.

6. Ibid.

7. Goldblatt, Henry. "Cisco's secrets," *Fortune*, August 11, 1999.

8. Ibid.

9. Daly, James. "The art of the deal," *Business 2.0*, October 1999.

10. Werbach, Kevin. "How big companies respond," in Release 1.0, EDventure Holdings, New York, NY, January 2000.

11. Op. cit.

s i x

[structuring for webs of innovation]

GREAT YOU MIGHT THINK. YOU UNDERSTAND THE WHY BEHIND
the struggle of established companies and immature markets. The
markets of established companies, mature markets, have different
innovation processes than immature markets where it is all about
networked innovation. In immature markets you have to make sure
you're part of webs of innovation by internal venturing, corporate
venture capital, and acquisitions. If established companies want to
become dot corps they should make sure they plug themselves into the
relevant webs of innovation via networked innovation so they can
make it in the internet evolution. So far so good. But how can a
company structure for webs of innovation?

Unfortunately, there isn't a magic formula yet. Established companies
have not found the best way to structure this networked innovation. In
this chapter you will learn why separation is the name of the game and

One of the

separate new

is that the

might

the existing

reasons to businesses new business cannibalize business.

how some companies are giving it a try in a way that they think best fits the organization. Some companies even combine all networked innovation activities under one "umbrella" in so-called networked innovation nodes. We will have an in-depth look at Volvo as an example of a company that has set up its networked innovation node.

The need for separation

In the eighties IBM was leading in the mainframe sector while something new was emerging in the computer industry; the personal computer (PC). The first PC came from a new start-up called Apple. At IBM it became clear that this PC might become a threat. IBM responded by creating a separate unit dedicated to starting IBM's PC business. To make sure that it could develop without conflicts with the existing businesses the unit was organizationally and physically separated, far away from the company's headquarters in Armonk, New York, the PC unit was started in Boca Raton in Florida. From there on it successfully developed into one of IBM's business units.

Why is this separation needed? Because innovation in mature markets is a different process than networked innovation, or innovation in an immature market. Putting networked innovation in a mature market environment can kill it. As a senior executive at a well-known public European high tech company told me "New business + old business = costly old business."

One of the reasons to separate new businesses is that the new business might cannibalize the existing business. Because of this, it is preferable not to have that new business in the same environment as the existing business as that part of the organization might perceive the cannibalization potential as a threat and try to kill it. For the company to survive sometimes giving businesses that might cannibalize existing business a chance is key for strategic renewal. To make sure the company retains its market share in a changing market, sometimes cannibalizing existing products might be needed, because at the end of the day a company wants to have the biggest share in its market and not for a certain product – especially if that product is made obsolete by a new product.

Canon for example launched its inkjet printers despite the damage to the company's dominant position in laser printers. That way Canon remained a leader in the printer market, because at the end of the day that is what the company wanted to be, not the leader in the laser printing market at all costs. "It's better to shoot yourself in the foot than have your competitor aiming for your head" the saying goes in Silicon Valley.

Another interesting case that showed the importance of isolation is that of Kodak's experience with electronic imaging. Initially the electronic imaging related activities were structured under the company's chemical imaging facilities. Managers of the film business continually interfered with the electronic imaging business as they perceived it as threatening to the existing customer base. As the operations were spread over the units this resulted in a lack of a clear strategy and measurement of success. With the arrival of a new CEO, George Fisher, all electronic imaging activities were put in one autonomous division.[1]

Another reason for separation is that it allows for optimal interaction with the relevant webs of innovation. An environment is needed that allows for an external focus and a certain autonomy to operate quickly and flexibly within these webs of innovation. With new businesses, structure should be following strategy instead of the reverse.

In the past, efforts have been made to enable this via the business unit structure.[2] However, in practice as the structure from established companies is based on current and/or core business, the focus is on efficiency. Business units develop their business and do research based on existing businesses. That way there is a low willingness to fund projects outside of existing business. Something completely new therefore gets rejected as it does not fit "the company way," also called the "not invented here" syndrome.

In practice change seems to be a top down thing. Change happens only when top management accepts it and takes the necessary steps to reorganize the company and so adapt the structure to the new organization. This is not an organic process as it always seems to happen in waves. It might be announced as a reorganization to make sure the organizational structure matches the changed market conditions, but in practice, it is proof that a company missed a new wave and has to catch up.

The pattern of missing new waves always seems to be the same. An organizational structure fits a company as it grows and becomes mature. When the market is changed, by disruptive technologies or another external cause, the structure that made it a success is often behind a slow death as the company is too slow to catch up and adapt to the new circumstances. Somehow it seems as though this is an irreversible path. As companies become mature, they attract people who like such an environment and slowly the innovative spirit dies. With that the strategic renewal competences die as well. However, companies are increasingly aware of this and acknowledge the importance of networked innovation for strategic renewal by starting and structuring networked innovation activities to enter the relevant webs of innovation on time, to ensure they make it through the internet evolution and become dot corps.

With networked innovation, the web of innovation should be the starting point, not strategy or structure. New stuff often comes from new entrants, spin-offs of established companies or by established companies entering a new business. As the developments in a concept are continuous and fast, participants in a web of innovation have to adapt continuously at the same speed internally. To an outsider it might even seem chaotic. It is not something that fits in an existing business environment that is based on stable and mature markets. These companies focus on having a dominant position in a few key markets instead of focusing on being part of a web of innovation and making sure they are early leaders in new markets.

For networked innovation an environment is needed where there is a leaning towards getting things done fast. That requires an open minded environment where people who best fit with networked innovation are tolerated. These are usually intrapreneurial people with a passion for the company who can think out of the box about long-term strategy, even if it involves cannibalizing an existing business. Greater emphasis should therefore be placed on facilitating this environment with the appropriate incentives and capital than on structuring it too much. Management awareness is key. Table 6.1 contains an overview of the characteristics that networked innovation should be kept free of.

With networked innovation, the web of innovation should be the starting point, not strategy or structure.

Table 6.1 Escaping the established business environment

Away from	Towards
Intellectual arrogance (the "not invented here" syndrome)	Being open minded
Slow decision making	Fast decision making
Low willingness to fund projects outside the scope of existing business	Willingness to try something new ("out of the box" thinking)
Structuring for control	Facilitating in a structured way
Fear of cannibalizing existing current products	Being able to "shoot in the foot"
Lack of top management attention	Top management awareness
Top management isolation	Orientation to the market
Intolerance of fanatics	Tolerating experts/fanatics
Short-time horizons	Long-time horizons
High early costs	Low early costs
Accounting practices	Availability of capital
Excessive rationalism	Need/achievement orientation
Excessive bureaucracy	Small, flat organization and developmental short cuts
No recognition	Incentive

Source: Quinn (1985) and author's findings

The importance of separating networked innovation is increasingly acknowledged, although companies are still figuring out a way to do this. As Harvard Business School Professor and author of bestseller *The Innovator's Dilemma*, Clayton Christensen told me: "There is no best way yet. Companies have not found a vehicle yet to deal with this networked innovation."

As I argued earlier in this chapter you should not structure for control of networked innovation. However, you can facilitate it in a structured way, making sure the appropriate and separate environment is provided. Many established companies are slowly starting to acknowledge that and are giving it a try. However, all of this still has to prove itself. One evident pattern is that an increasing number of established companies are setting up a separate subsidiary for their networked innovation activities; networked innovation nodes.

Networked innovation nodes

A study by strategic consulting firm Booz, Allen & Hamilton found that of companies active in networked innovation they researched about 74 percent had established a separate subsidiary or division for networked innovation.[3] Only 17 percent embedded these activities within an existing business unit or division. Nine percent created a hybrid, combining in-house capabilities with a separate subsidiary or division.

Many of these companies are setting up what I would like to call networked innovation nodes. These are separate parts of the organization that are comprised of all networked innovation activities. These networked innovation nodes have not been around too long with the majority of companies that have them, so they are all experimenting with finding the right way to do things. They have not worked out the right way yet. But all of them acknowledge the importance of networked innovation nodes as the best way to hook up with webs of innovation without being slowed down by the existing business. It might be that over time all companies have networked innovation nodes composed of an internal venturing program, a CVC fund, and an acquisitions team.

For internal

add value to

business, the

invest in and

start-ups

ventures that the core divisions nurture these themselves.

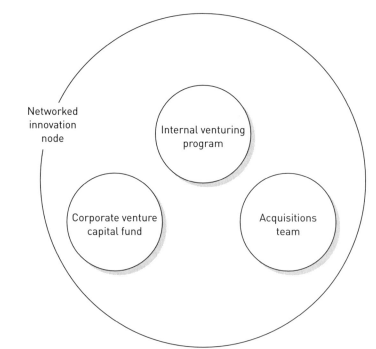

FIGURE 6.1 The networked innovation node

However, it's not all that rigid. Reuters for instance has a CVC fund, the Greenhouse fund that also invests in internal ventures. It only invests in internal ventures that dovetail with the rest of its portfolio. For internal ventures that add value to the core business, the divisions invest in and nurture these start-ups themselves.

Lucent has chosen another approach. Besides its internal venturing program mentioned in Chapter 3, it also has a CVC fund called "Lucent Venture Partners." Steve Socolof, VP Lucent New Ventures Group, told me that both these groups are separate because of the different nature of these activities. The New Ventures Group primarily focuses on ideas from *within* Lucent and is actively involved in turning these ideas into businesses. Lucent Venture Partners focuses on ideas outside of Lucent and in which it takes minority shares as a passive investor (see Table 6.2).

TABLE 6.2 The New Ventures Group versus Lucent Venture Partners

	New Ventures Group	Lucent Venture Partners
Organization	Lucent Business Group	Lucent subsidiary
Primary source of venture ideas/new products	From within Lucent	From outside of Lucent
Venture organization model(s)	Internal ventures External ventures	External ventures
Participation in Ventures	Active in establishing and leading business ventures	Passive minority investor

What is the best format differs for each company, although several companies have put their networked innovation key components in one unit. Chapter 4 described Nokia's networked innovation node, the Nokia Ventures Organization, for example. For internal ideas that do not fit within the existing businesses Nokia has an internal venturing program called the Entrepreneurial Web. Nokia has defined three new business areas – Nokia Internet Communications, Nokia Home Communications, and Nokia Mobile Display Appliances, which are explored and developed by these ventures. Nokia Venture Partners complements the organization by investing in external ventures in the wireless space to keep in touch with new webs of innovation. The Nokia Ventures Organization is a business unit of Nokia.

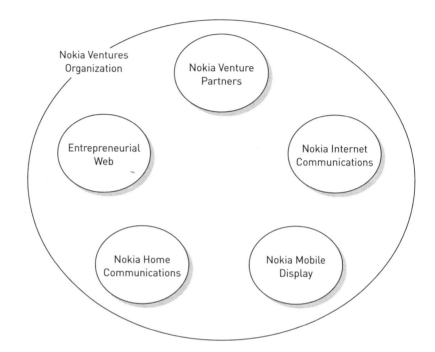

FIGURE 6.2 Nokia's networked innovation node

Another interesting example is that of KPN Valley. Netherlands-based KPN, a telecoms company, has been active in the past with acquisitions, venture capital, and similar initiatives but also has been confronted with talented employees leaving the organization to start their own ventures. To structure its networked innovation activities the company set up a separate legal entity in 2000 called "KPN Valley." It integrates KPN Ventures (its VC fund), an incubator and a so-called "convergence idea generator" where ideas are worked out in collaboration with external parties. One idea that came out of the convergence idea generator was the Convergence Fund, a $30 million VC fund of publisher VNU and KPN. The incubator is also open to ventures that originate from outside of KPN.

In an interview KPN Valley executive Rob Langezaal gives two reasons for having KPN Valley:[4]

● Real innovation should be in an environment that fits it best and which is separated from the existing business.

● To improve the processes that are already ongoing (KPN has been active in the past in CVC and acquisitions).

KPN Valley is also interesting because, as Langezaal emphasized, sponsorship of the ventures in KPN Valley by one of KPN's existing businesses is stimulated. This brings me to one of the main challenges faced by the networked innovation entities, that of tensions between their entity and the existing businesses part.

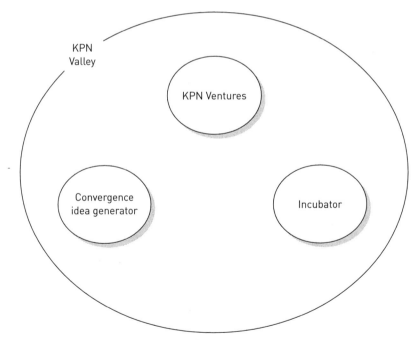

FIGURE 6.3 KPN's innovation node

The existing businesses might be hesitant to share the attractive assets such as brand, distribution channels, and so on with the networked innovation nodes out of a self-protection instinct. Middle management within established companies can often be reluctant to collaborate as there is no incentive for them to collaborate. Not being able to offer or having problems in delivering the added value an established company offers can kill its success. The same is true of attracting versus retaining top talent. The existing business part might be annoyed that talented employees are being attracted by the challenges and rewards offered by the networked innovation node. Therefore the executive in charge needs to be somebody with an intrapreneurial mindset, combining entrepreneurial characteristics with political skills. It is for this reason that such executives tend to be recruited from within the company. They often have been with the company for a long while and have held senior positions within the company. Within the structure, the executive usually reports directly to the CEO. The executive of Volvo Technology Transfer AB (see below), for instance reports directly to the CEO. The support of the CEO and other executives is key. If they do not see the importance of networked innovation there is no use in structuring the activities. The company should commit to clear goals related to networked innovation, e.g. deriving at least two new businesses ideas per year from networked innovation. At 3M for instance the goal is to produce 30 percent of its annual sales from products that are less than four years old. Ten percent of sales is expected from products less than one year old.[5]

There is probably no single best way but there will be *best practice* examples of companies that know how to succesfully deal with networked innovation. At the end of the day, it's about results. After the internet evolution, success will be measured by whether established companies have become dot corps.

The executive in charge needs to be somebody with an intrapreneurial mindset, combining entrepreneurial characteristics with political skills.

It is clear that it is best to separate networked innovation from the rest of the organization because of its different nature. It might be that over time companies will have "networked innovation nodes" comprised of one or more of the key components of networked innovation. Volvo is one company that has set up its networked innovation node.

Volvo Technology Transfer AB

In 1984, Volvo's then CEO, Pehr G. Gyllenhammar, founded the European Round Table, consisting of the 25 largest European companies at the time. They created a venture capital fund called Euroventures and put in $250 million which was then a vast amount of money in the European VC market. Volvo's Rutger Friberg was responsible for the fund, although his main job was corporate strategy and planning. Stimulated by this initiative Volvo formed the Volvo Venture Management department in 1996, which took care of Volvo's interests in the VC field, and Friberg headed it.

In 1997 Volvo started the Volvo Technology Transfer (VTT) AB as a subsidiary to AB Volvo. The goal was threefold:

- to identify and spin-off business from Volvo;

- to invest in external technology and competence with potential for Volvo's core activities;

● to promote and develop innovator- and entrepreneurships within Volvo.

Within the structure of Volvo, VTT was meant to be complementary to the Volvo Technical Development Corporation. Besides being a link to the external environment, it brings technology or competence to places where it is useful and also promotes co-operation within the Volvo Group. The company has recruited Anders Brännström as an external CEO. He has experience of Mergers and Acquisitions and other relevant skills. The reason was that it would help to get the company off to a flying start. Friberg is now Senior Vice President (SVP).

The reason for having the unit separated was, according to Friberg, "One main advantage to have it this way is the short leadtime from idea to investment decision via our own board for VTT. Another is that we do not have to spend a lot of time to seek funding."

VTT is staffed by seven people; a CEO, a SVP, a secretary, and four investment managers.

In practice, the threefold goal has lead to the following achievements:

● participation in pooled funds in Sweden, Europe, and US (500 million SEK = approximately $58 million, December 1999);

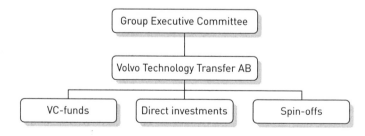

FIGURE 6.4 Volvo Technology Transfer AB organizational structure

- direct investments, seed, and later stages; 20 investments made (December 1999);

- spin-offs (mainly development projects that have generated products or methods or business ideas that are besides the core business).

Determinants of an interesting investment (direct investment or spin-off) for Volvo include:

- a possible sales potential of more than 200 million SEK (approximately $23 million);

- additional market potential outside the Volvo customer base;

- relevance to the Volvo Group;

- possibility to ensure competent management with good track record;

- strategic fit.

Employees who participate in a spin-off receive part of the company, a bonus, or options. Since European tax laws are less entrepreneur friendly than in the US, the option often depends on the tax position.

VTT has a board that is authorized to make decisions regarding investments in new companies. In the case of direct investments or spin-offs VTT sometimes wants a place on the board. Volvo also places acquired companies in VTT to let it act as an incubator and to transfer them in a later stage either to exit (and gain ROI) or to incorporate them in the main structure.

Neither VTT nor the rest of the Volvo Group has an internal venturing program.

It is too early to be able to state whether Volvo has been successful or not with Volvo Technology Transfer AB. However, it is one example of a company that is trying to facilitate networked innovation in a structured way by setting up a networked innovation node.

The future

Although networked innovation nodes are in a very early stage and time will reveal how well these nodes work, there are already some interesting things going on. The webs of innovation that networked innovation nodes are involved in can quickly outgrow the organization.

The number of employees of all the companies in Reuters' Greenhouse Fund portfolio for instance, equals the number of Reuters employees (17,000). Its contribution to the Reuters group profits grew to 9 percent in about five years. You might think that this is still a small percentage. However, don't forget that Reuters has been around since 1850 and the Reuters Greenhouse Fund only since 1995.

The interesting thing with the Reuters Greenhouse Fund is that because of its successes with the fund, a large web of innovation has developed. As Reuters only takes minority stakes, it does not have a powerful position. It cannot control the web of innovation it has woven. Within the web, companies connect with each other and with other webs and so on. It could be speculated that one day Reuters might become a portfolio company of the Reuters Greenhouse Fund or that one of the portfolio companies makes Reuters become obsolete.

What can be learned from the Reuters example is that the networked innovation node might change companies into formats that best suit life after the internet evolution. For Reuters that might be a web-based organization.

Although many companies are just beginning to structure networked innovation, it will be interesting to see how the networked innovation nodes help the transition towards new organizational structures and what these new organizational structures will look like.

Conclusion
As networked innovation is different from innovation in existing businesses, it is best to separate it from the existing business. There does not yet seem to be one best way for structuring for networked innovation. It seems that there is a trend towards putting all networked innovation key components in a separate unit, a networked innovation node.

What is becoming clear is that by increasingly structuring networked innovation, companies are trying to master innovation by entering webs of innovation. With the internet as one of the most disruptive technologies to date, the established companies are made extra aware of the importance of networked innovation as they missed out in the internet revolution. With the internet evolution they have a second chance to become dot corps, and this is an even more interesting opportunity as the real money will be made in the second wave. It is up to the established companies to prove themselves and make it to being dot corps.

If established companies undertake networked innovation in the right way and get into the relevant webs of innovation that might be the route for them to become dot corps and master innovation.

As networked

different from

in existing

it is best to

from **the**

innovation is innovation businesses, separate it existing business.

Key points

 How are networked innovation activities structured within your organization?

 Should networked innovation activities be separate from the main business?

 If there is no structure in place, how could your company organize for innovation without losing sight of today's performance?

 How does the management team acknowledge the importance of networked innovation?

 How many business plans for new ideas reaches senior management in your company every year?

 How can you operationalize networked innovation and bring it to life?

 What is the relationship between the networked innovation activities in your company and the existing businesses?

 How is networked innovation managed in your company? Is there a long-term strategy?

 How can ongoing commitment to networked innovation be assured?

 How can you leverage your (perhaps limited) innovation resources?

Further information

At the website **www.websofinnovation.com** you can find additional resources on the subject, such as links to relevant articles, books, websites and this will be expanded over time. A mailing list on the subject of this chapter allows you to discuss it with other readers.

Notes

1. Day, George and Schoemaker, Paul. "Don't hesitate to innovate," *Financial Times*, October 9, 2000.

2. Chandler, 1962.

3. Albrinck, Jill *et al.* "Adventures in corporate venturing," *Strategy+Business*, First quarter 2001, Issue 22, New York, NY.

4. Doorenbosch, Thijs. "KPN 'koopt' inspiratie met risicogeld voor starters," *Automatiseringsgids*, November 3, 2000.

5. Leifer, Richard *et al. Radical innovation; how mature companies can outsmart upstarts*, Harvard Business School Press, Cambridge 2000.

s e v e n

[epilog: will dot corps be webs?]

THE INTERNET WILL CHANGE THE WORLD. THERE IS NO DOUBT
about that. However, we are in a really early stage. Think about it, to
what extent has your daily live really changed since the arrival of the
internet? It's "scene I, act II" and nobody really knows what the
internet is going to bring us in the long term. As with all major
disruptive technologies it takes time to become mature and accepted.
For example, 40 years elapsed between the invention of electricity and
its adoption by the majority of industries. After revolution comes
evolution.

Companies that do not adapt during the evolution might become
dinosaurs and be replaced by a new player. The internet revolution
woke up the established companies that they have to change to adapt
to the Information Age by becoming dot corps, otherwise they might
become dinosaurs. Via networked innovation activities such as internal

Networked nodes might be towards the new from controlling hierarchical facilitating a customers, employees and innovation the first step model; moving an efficient structure to network of partners, competitors.

venturing, corporate venture capital, and acquisitions, these established companies try to become dot corps. Although in the internet revolution the start-ups ruled, the established companies seem to be striking back in the internet evolution. This time start-ups are joining forces with established companies to help them become dot corps via webs of innovation.

So far established companies are trying to work on setting up and structuring their networked innovation based activities to become dot corps without knowing how this dot corp is going to be like. Networked innovation nodes might be the first step towards the new model; a web based one. From controlling an efficient hierarchical structure to facilitating a network of customers, partners, employees, and competitors. Not a hierarchical, closed pyramid structure but a web in which the established company is the glue that holds the web together. The coming years will reveal more about what the dot corps will look like.

No dot corps blueprint

There is no blueprint available for a dot corp. There is consensus, however, that a new structure is coming up as society is starting to change. We're moving from an industrial age towards the information age.

There seems to be an increasing awareness that things are changing. During the internet revolution there was an overreaction but even now, after the internet hype is over the awareness is still there. Several communities have formed which offer a place to think and learn about things to come. One of the more well-known examples is the magazine *Fast Company*. This US publication has been around since 1995 and describes how companies and the people behind them are dealing with the transition. It also organizes events and has worldwide meetings in cities (*Fast Company* "cell of friends"), creating a global community of people interested in things changing. They call it a movement. On a smaller scale there are several similar communities emerging that are interested in the changes. But what is it that is changing?

In the industrial age machines took over certain tasks done before by humans which brought us the current organizational structures. In the information age information is made increasingly accessible; for more people, faster and easier. That requires different organizational structures than the current organizational structures that were an outcome of the industrial age and were based on a scarcity of information.

In the industrial age companies were about control. People that had access to the most information were in control, i.e. management and shareholders. In the information age information is no longer a scarce resource and is not, therefore, a source of power. Employees, partners, competitors, and customers are becoming increasingly powerful because information is easier and faster to access for them. The emphasis for established companies seems to move from controlling an efficient hierarchical structure to facilitating a network of customers, partners, employees, and competitors. Not a hierarchical closed pyramid structure but a web in which the established company is the glue that holds the web together.

Within these webs, information is the oil that makes the machine work. Not capital or ownership as in the industrial age type of organization. It is now important to be well informed so that the right connections can be made. It is not a *structure focused* approach but a *process focused* one.

That leads to some completely different characteristics of the structure. The web is an open system that is in continuous interaction with its environment. Because of its structure, it is easy to adapt to its environment; it is self organizing. A different organizational structure than the ones you see nowadays.

However, the danger with talking about this is that you end up in theory. At the end of the day it is still speculation. Organizations are not yet structured in this way. Over time we will see how this unproven model proves itself in practice. It might also be that a structure will emerge that we had not previously thought of. Meanwhile in the real world established companies are just making their first moves towards becoming dot corps.

One thing is sure – that organizational structures might change but not everything is changing as radically as "new" economy evangelists thought a couple of years ago. Change takes time.

In the euphoric atmosphere of the internet revolution it was believed that everything was going to change radically. All things existing would be made obsolete. Business principles that had been around for ages were assumed to have become irrelevant. "Clear your brain of all you've learned as the internet will challenge all you've learned" it seemed. Established companies were based on these old principles and would therefore not make it into the "new" economy. Small flexible start-ups would, with a fresh view, take over all existing industries, make the existing players obsolete, and start a new world. However, now these start-ups are struggling to survive and established companies are making their first moves towards becoming dot corps. It seems that the established companies are striking back in the internet evolution.

How to become a dot corp

It turned out that it was not without reason that most of the previously challenged business principles have been around for so long. They are *true*. The start-ups found this out for themselves as many had a hard time building a profitable and sustainable business. Meanwhile all the bragging by the start-ups had woken up the established companies. They started to buy-in to the fact that the internet was something that would change the world and would require a different role and organizational structure for established companies; a dot corp. How should they adapt and become dot corps?

Established companies do not have a good track record in strategic renewal and there are numerous examples of companies that missed out on disruptive waves. When active in mature markets established companies seem to thrive. However, remaining a leading position in an existing market and meanwhile making sure that new immature markets rise and that they participate in these has been hard for established companies. Mature markets differ from immature markets. These immature market start with a concept around which a web of innovation involving customers, competitors, and partners evolves. That requires a different approach than the existing business approach.

As I quoted in Chapter 1, John Chambers, CEO of Cisco, wrote me "You bring up an interesting point about mature markets versus. immature markets ... [networked innovation] includes partnering, acquisitions and internal and external investments as the goal is to be best in class at various levels and to create an 'ecosystem' of partners."

Acknowledging the different approaches needed for immature and mature markets, an increasing number of established companies is trying to deal with these immature markets by entering webs of innovation via networked innovation; internal venturing, corporate venture capital, and acquisitions. This is especially true of the established companies that might face threats in their industry as the internet might disrupt it.

Innovation markets is a process than mature markets. separate

in immature

different

innovation in

so it is best to

the two.

As these networked innovation nodes grow and some of them become successful they might lay the foundations for the new organization. Schwab, for example, merged its existing business into the new one, eSchwab. A more radical example is Reuters networked innovation node; the Reuters Greenhouse Fund. One day the Reuters Greenhouse Fund might outgrow the Reuters Group, meaning that the organization becomes a web-based one.

During the internet revolution established companies saw talented companies leaving to create new companies, often based on ideas perceived while being an employee, and creating huge value as the Ericsson example in Chapter 3 showed. Unfortunately for the established companies they never benefited in any way from these gains. To avoid this and not to miss out on the internet evolution established companies are increasingly starting internal venturing programs. In Chapter 3 I described the Lucent New Ventures Group. In practice, setting up these internal venturing programs proves to be difficult, however, and has let to the rise of e-builders – companies helping established companies to set up their e-ventures. All these programs are as young as the ventures they are nurturing so therefore it is hard to state whether they have been successful. Most internal venturing programs are still refining their strategies as they grow. Over time we will know which approaches were successful and which were not.

To stay in touch with the market and see new webs of innovation emerging that have a disruptive potential but also to promote the company's products within these webs of innovation, established companies are increasingly active in corporate venture capital. Intel for instance uses corporate venture capital to stimulate the sales of its chips. The growth of corporate venture capital has especially been stimulated with the arrival of the internet. The percentage of deals involving corporate venture capital grew from 9 percent in 1994 to 27 percent in 2000 according to VentureOne. As the hype is over, start-ups are starting to appreciate the tangible and intangible assets of the established companies. Established companies tend to have different ways to structure corporate venture capital but the separate entity seems to prevail.

During the hype the initial public offering was the preferred exit strategy for most start-ups. However, companies are finding that it takes time to build a profitable and sustainable business. Established companies can help accelerate the growth when they acquire these companies. All of this has led to an increase in the number of acquisitions. During the hype companies were started with the objective of making the established companies become obsolete. In practice it turns out that there have not so far been that many start-ups which have made established companies become obsolete. Now it seems the contrary is happening. Instead of taking on established companies creating companies that help them become dot corps is becoming the theme of start-ups in the Internet evolution. As established companies are increasingly acquiring start-ups they are structuring and standardizing the process; Cisco is a good example of that.

Innovation in immature markets is a different process than innovation in mature markets, so it is best to separate the two. An increasing number of companies are setting up separate parts of their organization, networked innovation nodes, in which they facilitate the key components of networked innovation. How that is done differs in each company, but it is clearly a trend. Over time it will become clear which ways of setting up networked innovation nodes have been most effective to help established companies become dot corps. Examples of networked innovation nodes I discussed in Chapter 6 are Nokia, KPN, and Volvo.

The overall result seems to be that it is no longer a question of start-ups trying to beat the established companies as in David versus Goliath but that they have found each other in webs of innovation. Both doing what they are good at; start-ups in creating competences and established companies turning these into businesses. Start-ups are helping established companies to become dot corps. David and Goliath joining forces in webs of innovation.

The first signs of this are already showing. Instead of attacking the established companies, start-ups are turning to offer the technologies they developed to established companies. Business-to-business companies are for instance offering their software to established companies that enables them to create their own marketplaces. Using the competences developed by start-ups these established companies are already on the way to becoming dot corps. Many established companies have already changed the way they deal with their customers and suppliers. They seem to be striking back in the internet

Benefiting from extra channel to business is just

evolution. Only for the first step in the Internet evolution though. Benefiting from the Internet as an extra channel to improve your business. That's just the start.

To avoid missing out on the next steps or their industry being disrupted, leaving them out, it is essential to enter actively the right webs of innovation if established companies want to become dot corps.

What will these dot corps look like? Nobody knows yet; it might be in web form, or it might be quite different. Nobody knows. One thing everybody agrees on is that things are starting to change as we are moving from the industrial age to the information age. In this evolutional phase, companies that miss out become dinosaurs. Networked innovation makes sure established companies do not miss out in the internet evolution to make it to the information age. This book has shown you how companies are starting to do that. I hope it has been of help with structuring your thoughts. Now the question to consider is; how will *your* company become a dot corp?

the internet as an improve your the start.

index